COMBAT MASTER

Sid Woodcock and Detonics

By Allen J. Chinn

Also from Allen J. Chinn

A Kung-Fu Master's Journey

Kung-Fu Table Tennis

Rebirth from the Ashes

Bad Cut

Ladies Fight Back

2012 The Beginning

Please visit www.allenchinn.com.

COMBAT MASTER

ISBN: 978-1-105-48076-8

Disclaimer: This work is a memoir. It reflects the author's present recollection of his experiences and stories told to him, over a period of many years.

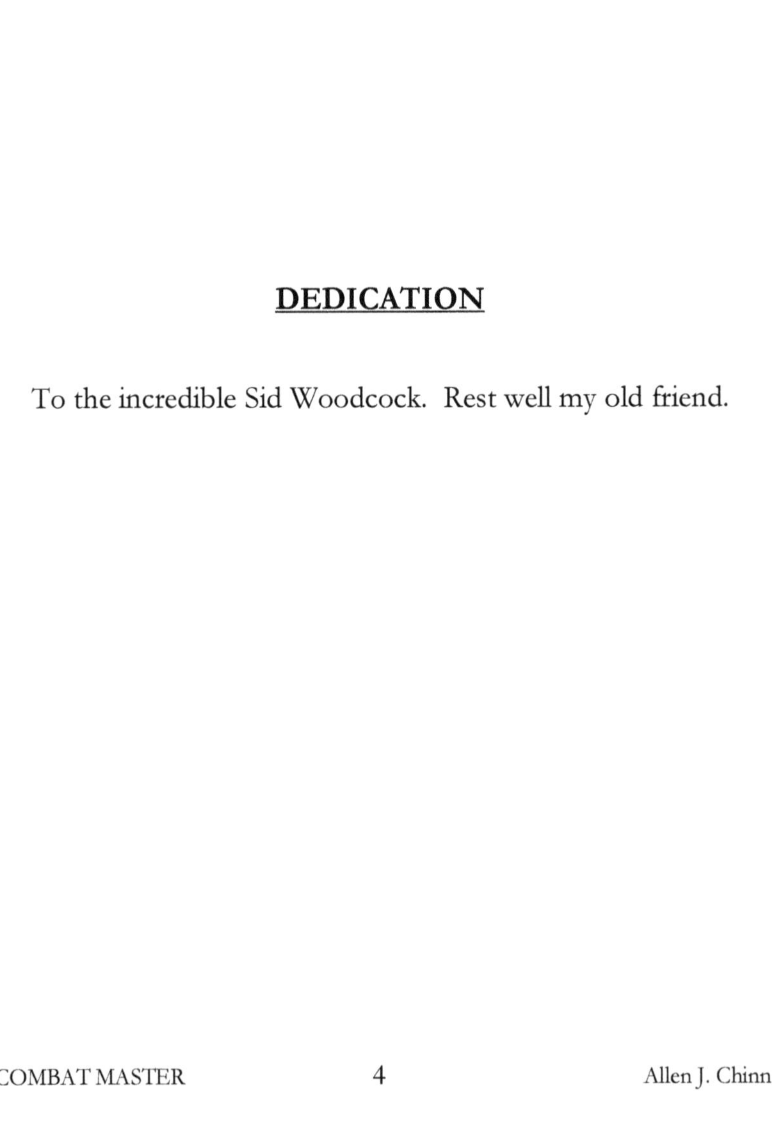

DEDICATION

To the incredible Sid Woodcock. Rest well my old friend.

ACKNOWLEDGEMENTS

Melissa Chow for her outstanding graphic design work.

Robert Mosebar (Sid Woodcock's son) for the use of his father's pictures.

Bruce Siddle and Detonics Defense, Doug Barnes, Peter Dunn, Richard Niemer, Chuck McGough, and Steven Chinn for their pictures and support.

PREFACE

I was shocked and deeply saddened when I heard that my dear friend Sid Woodcock had passed away. I had just visited him on his 87th birthday and it was unknown to me that he passed away just a week later.

Our friendship was special. It began 28 years ago with him hiring me as the Technical Representative for the Sales and Marketing Department of Detonics Manufacturing Corporation. Sid was the President of the company. We had an instant connection as our passion for firearms and the martial arts were very similar.

If I told you that there was a person that was one of the early 1940s OSS (Office of Strategic Services) operatives and later worked under contract for the CIA (Central Intelligence Agency), Atomic Energy Commission, Department of Defense, FBI (Federal Bureau of Investigation), Secret Service and the Department of Justice; trained at Shaolin during World War II, trained at the Kodokan in Japan after World War II, was a Grandmaster of Chin Na, 8th Degree Black Belt in Shinobi, instructor of units from the U.S. Army Special Forces and U.S. Navy Seal Teams, taught Bruce Lee joint locking techniques; an expert in firearms and explosives, and a watch maker you would think I was crazy or a liar.

Sid was all of these things and more. He was friends with early 1940s mixed martial arts instructors Lieutenant-Colonel William E. Fairbairn (British Secret Service) and Colonel Rex Applegate (Office of Strategic Services). He was also friends with Lieutenant-Colonel Jeff Cooper, the "father" of modern pistolcraft, as well as former CIA Director William J. Casey. His list of friends of notoriety would be indeed staggering if we could have done all the research prior to his passing.

Sid was like "Forrest Gump" as he would show up everywhere, throughout history. He was living it as he was making it. Imagine he started fighting for our freedoms over two generations ago.

He was a very special unsung hero. His work in covert and classified operations would keep his family and friends in a cloud of mystery and uncertainty. That was the nature of his work. His sacrifice to his country would be his priority.

This book is my memoir of my friend Sid Woodcock and Detonics. Sid's background insured that the Detonics Combat Master was a pistol fit for impossible missions. Sid and the pistol that he made famous were indeed Combat Masters.

TABLE OF CONTENTS

CHAPTER 1

My History with Martial Arts and Firearms 1964-1982

Martial Arts

I started training in Chinese martial arts in 1964. I was 8 years old and received my interest in the police and detective shows of the time. No one really knew martial arts in those shows of the day, but I was fascinated with the ability to take out people with a single "Judo" chop, or knee to the groin.

My father was an expert in Choy Li Fut Kung-Fu. So I trained with him, learning basic stances, blocks and strikes. Years later I started to add techniques of my friends. I incorporated facets of Hung-Ga, Wing Chun, and Northern Mantis Kung-Fu.

During the summer of 1973, I was 16 years old and with the prompting of my sister Susan, I taught a Kung-Fu class at the University of Washington's Experimental College.

When I was 17 years old, Bruce Lee was a martial arts phenomenon. His philosophy influenced my own training and combat ideology. He believed in discarding the "classical mess" and absorbing what was useful.

I believed that there was a middle ground where what was classical that worked, was indeed as valuable as non-classical/modern that worked. I also believed that seldom seen techniques offered an advantage to overcome those that could not understand them, or cope with them.

The summer of 1974 I taught a Kung-Fu class for Seattle Parks and Recreation at the Jefferson Community Center.

In 1975 I had created a devastating, effective martial art. It is based on classical/non-classical Chinese martial arts techniques. It incorporated numerous drills to give the students increased speed, reflexes, strength and power. The style would incorporate classical movements that would permit the student to compete on any level in classical forms competitions. It incorporated modern training ideas so students could compete in the sport aspect of the martial arts.

However, it never lost its true combative nature. The martial arts are a way of life. The training of severe and deadly techniques is knowledge that is not intended to be used, but can be called upon in serious emergencies. Practice is the training of the body and the mind. When everything "fits" it becomes part of you, part of your spirit.

From the classical styles you could train in traditional and seldom seen animal techniques, strikes, blocks, kicks, joint locks, seizing, flexible weaponry, bladed weaponry, staffs of all kinds, etc…

I called this style Yee Jong Kune Do. The way of the internal combination fist.

In the fall of 1975 I was teaching a couple of students privately at the Green River Community College. Soon after this I taught at a school in Puyallup that was named the South Hill Kung-Fu Institute.

In 1976 I took over my friend's Karate school and turned it into my Rainier Valley Kung-Fu school.

I taught in Kent in 1980. I also had a small school up on Beacon Hill that same year.

27 year old Sifu Allen J. Chinn at the 1983 Bellevue Kung-Fu Club

My Kung-Fu knowledge and ability has been a big part of me. It is and always had been a way of life for me. It is inseparable from the person that I have become.

I believe I have always trained for usage. I learned techniques that were to be used as they were intended. Various punches, strikes, kicks, blocks, etc... were only useful if they worked in combat.

In most Chinese martial arts, forms are important and are significant to each individual style. These forms provide the practitioner techniques to draw from. It is how the individual learns and develops those techniques that define their true understanding and ultimately their ability to use them in combat.

Without desiring a true understanding and ability to use a form for fighting purposes, the form is just a dance.

We can compare a martial arts form without combat understanding to dance (ballet, or jazz). Both display physical prowess, coordination and finesse. Neither has understanding of what physical damages their techniques can do. Neither train in striking, or kicking bags to develop more powerful techniques for greater combat effectiveness.

It is the desire to understand and have the ability to use the learned techniques in true combat that defines the individual.

Understanding a great variety of techniques that involve fistic, kicking, grappling, joint locking knowledge, as well as long weapons, short weapons, double weapons, flexible weapons, and shooting weapons, has always been my passion.

This passion for understanding what works, has given me the ability to find solutions in many directions.

I took all the techniques I had and learned if they were useful, and when they could be applied. Everything has its strengths, but everything also has its weaknesses.

The ability to defeat a formidable opponent starts with an open mind. Using varied attacks, counter-offenses, angles and techniques that they have little experience with, can be successful.

I opened my Bellevue Kung-Fu Club in the fall of 1982.

Firearms

I started my interest in firearms in 1964. I was 8 years old and this interest was also instilled in me by my father. I received a Spanish made AYA Matador, 20 gauge side by side shotgun and a Crosman 22 caliber air rifle from my father that year.

My father was an expert shot and was especially outstanding with a shotgun. He trained me in our basement shooting the air rifle at my plastic army men, or dinosaurs. My father had a very sturdy bullet trap made and that provided the safe backdrop to shoot downstairs. I loved shooting and hitting the plastic army men and dinosaurs and soon my father was complaining about how fast I was going through the 22 caliber pellets.

Since most all of his shooting involved hunting wild fowl my brother and I practiced with him out in the fields of Issaquah back in the mid 1960s through the mid 1970s. He had a heavy spring powered Outers clay pigeon thrower mounted on a long 2" by 10" plank. He would drive over the long plank with the front tire of his car and that would quickly anchor the clay pigeon thrower in a fixed, immovable position.

That is how we learned to shoot moving clay pigeons in flight. This would help us when we went hunting band-tailed pigeons, pheasants, or ducks.

My father used to subscribe to Field and Stream and Outdoor Life. These magazines highlighted fishing and hunting. I read these magazines from cover to cover. I was thoroughly immersed in each of the stories and learned the techniques and equipment used by the authors.

I got to be a very good wing shot and was successful at fishing also. I soon started showing interest in rifles and handguns too. My interest at outdoor sports continued to grow.

In 1975 I got a job as a sporting goods salesman at Jafco, a merchandising discount retailer. There I learned to mount scopes and install slings on rifles. I worked with numerous rifles and shotguns and my knowledge and experience increased.

As with my martial arts, I read everything I could get my hands on about various facets of the shooting sports. I read articles from Jack O'Connor, Jeff Cooper, Skeeter Skelton, Bob Milek, George Nonte, Col. Charles Askins and many others. My knowledge and understanding increased correspondingly.

I joined the Renton Fish and Game Club and practiced rifle and pistol shooting out there. I eventually shot on the shotgun side of the range also.

In 1977 I became the "Gun Man" at Fredericks and Nelson. This was a large department store and had a very impressive hunting and fishing department. I had the pleasure to work with the great gunsmiths Bill English and later Lloyd Erdman.

I also joined the Elliot Bay Pistol and Revolver Club. This was a private indoor handgun range located in Downtown Seattle on Western Street.

Part of my "perks" of the Fredericks and Nelson job was to have a presence at the Seattle Skeet and Trap Club. The store paid for my membership and paid for three rounds of trap and ammunition each week. I took advantage of this opportunity and became a fairly good competitive shot.

I was a NRA (National Rifle Association) Member. I also had memberships in the ATA (Amateur Trap Association) and P.I.T.A (Pacific International Trap Association). I also shot Continental Trap and International Skeet at the Seattle Skeet and Trap Club. I occasionally shot International Trap at the Renton Fish and Game Club.

I was in heaven. I shot trap and some skeet on Wednesday each week. I shot rifles and pistols on the weekends. Being young and living with my parents allowed me to have more money for reloading components. I was always trying to increase my skill and accuracy. I even shot an IPSC (International Practical Shooting Confederation) tournament in Vancouver, B.C. that year.

In 1978 I was hired by Washington Hardware to become a sales representative. Things did not go the way I planned so I left and was soon hired by Sportsland in Northgate, but only worked there two weeks before putting in my two week notice. I had interviewed and was hired to manage a gun shop in Auburn.

At Auburn Sports and Marine I was in charge of the gun department. In three years I took a small gun business from $30,000.00 a year, to over $1,000,000.00 annually. I took the small gun shop that focused only on fall hunting, to a busy year round business catering to combat sports, home defense and various types of target shooting in addition to hunting.

I created shooting contests that varied from bowling pins, balloons, flying clay pigeons and even a plastic bullet quick draw tournament. My clients were anyone that wanted to get better at shooting skills, hunters, IPSC competitors, silhouette competitors, self defense minded individuals and police officers.

In 1979 it was our shooting contest and this bowling pin shoot was the first in the Northwest region. I was able to draw in Northwest IPSC (International Practical Shooting Confederation) shooters, law enforcement officers and shooting enthusiasts to participate. Then IPSC President and Seattle Police Sergeant Dave Stanford participated and won the five pin concealed carry event, shooting his 5" 45 ACP 1911. Electrician Keith Ostlund won the single pin concealed carry event shooting his Dan Wesson 4" 357 magnum and former-Marine Bob Pelletier won the five pin any weapon event shooting my Remington 1100 12 gauge 22" auto.

At the gun shop I did minor gunsmithing in sight installations, trigger jobs, scope installations on rifles and handguns. I was responsible for the inventory purchases and creating the packages for sale.

Unfortunately due to the poor economic climate, the boat side of the business was not doing as well. The problem was the majority of the ongoing bills were on the boat side of the overall company. The boat side had row boats up to 25 foot luxury craft. They had full time staff that included two salespeople and three mechanics.

The owner decided to liquidate the gun business to keep his boats afloat. His wife also being his partner, did not like the self defense, combat and military type arms that heavily increased firearms sales anyway.

CHAPTER 2

Meeting Sid Woodcock

In 1983 I was running my Bellevue Kung-Fu Club, but I did not understand the complex nature of running a business with clients that could take long periods of time off for vacations and family trips. My income varied with the number of students gone on trips.

The Kung-Fu school was my contribution to the family coffers and my son was three years old. I would still look in the paper for work.

One day I saw that Detonics Manufacturing Corporation was hiring a person to be in their Sale and Marketing Department. I applied and was given an interview.

I personally owned several 1911 pistols and variations. I had also read the 1976 Guns and Ammo article written by Jeff Cooper about the amazing Detonics 45 ACP pistol.

I already had experience with cut down 1911 45 ACP pistols. In the mid 1970s my gunsmith friend Russ Field had made two cut down 1911s. He did this a few years earlier when he studied gunsmithing at Trinidad State Junior College. In fact Russ had even used one of them at Jim Gregg's point shooting school in 1975.

Photo of Detonics Combat Master cover in 1976

I knew that there had been several ways that gunsmiths had attempted to create the small, cut down 1911. Some had cut and welded the front of the slide. Some had built a bushing and threaded the front end of the shortened slide. Some gunsmiths even machined off the front locking lug of the barrel.

The Detonics Combat Master was unique as it was the smallest production 1911 ever made. Until its introduction, the Colt Combat Commander at 4.25" was the shortest available 1911 pistol. The innovative Detonics Combat Master was 3/4" shorter!

My knowledge of the features and the practical reasons for them would be an advantage for me.

I had several ideas on modifications that could enhance the 1911 full size, Commander length and the shortened Detonics length. Some of my drawings were for bowling pin competitions. The other ones were for better combat pistols.

Armed with these drawings, my resume and overall firearms knowledge, I was ready for my interview at Detonics.

I drove to the Bellevue facility. Going upstairs I was met by the office staff and they had me wait in another room. I was soon greeted by two men that entered the room. Sid introduced himself and Paul Marlow. Sid was the President of the company and Paul was one of the partners.

They both looked over my resume and then the drawings I had brought with me.

Paul commented, “I'm really impressed by these drawings! We always have a difficult time naming our guns. You have names for all these designs.”

Sid saw something in my resume that interested him. He asked, "So you're currently running a Kung-Fu school?" I answered "Yes." Then he asked where it was located and I told him it was right here in Factoria Square.

I seemed to have sufficiently impressed Sid and Paul and they hired me on the spot. My position would be on a probationary 3 month basis. If I passed the probation period, I would be brought on a permanent full time basis. They offered me a decent starting salary and included a "kit gun."

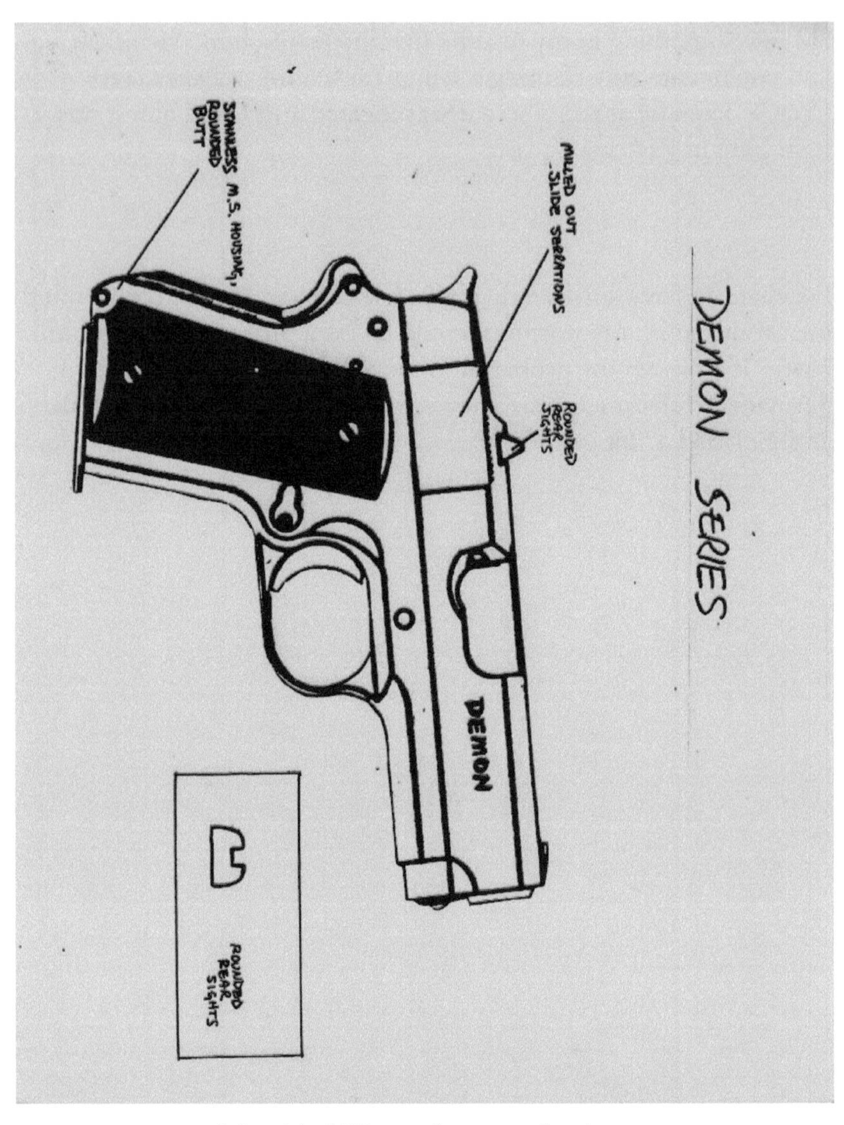

My original "Demon" concept drawing

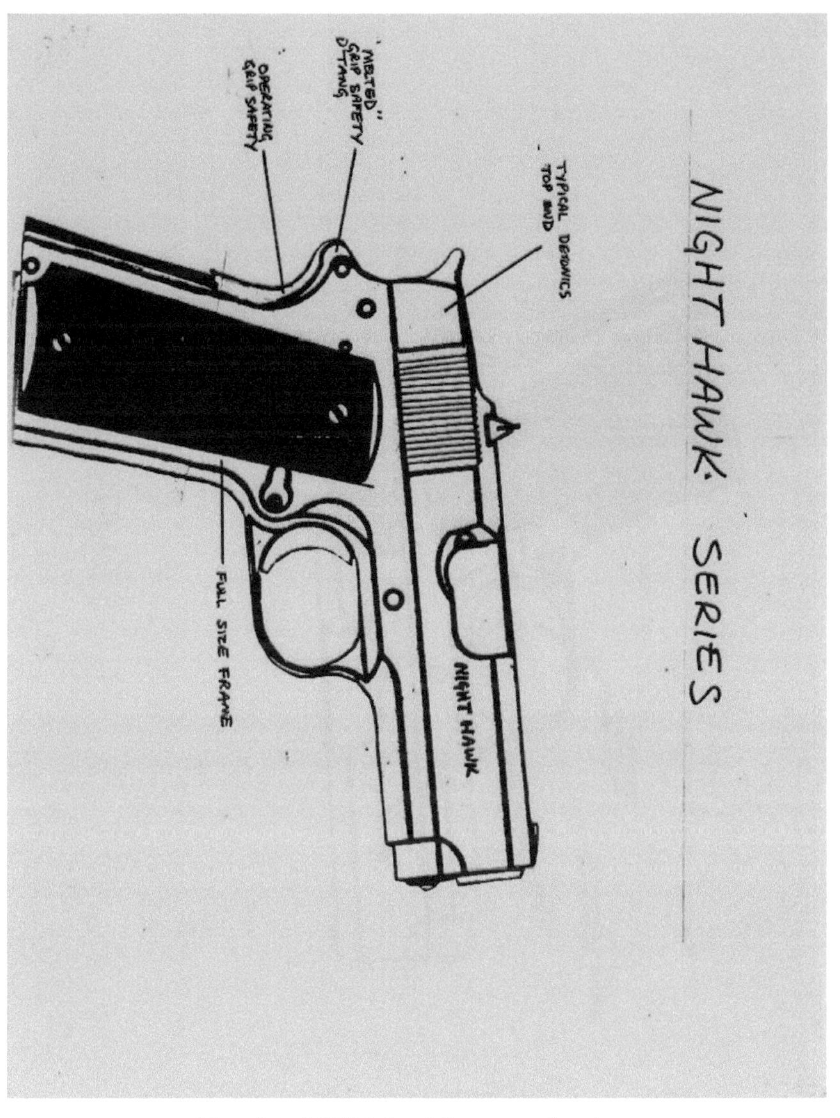

My original "Nighthawk" concept drawing

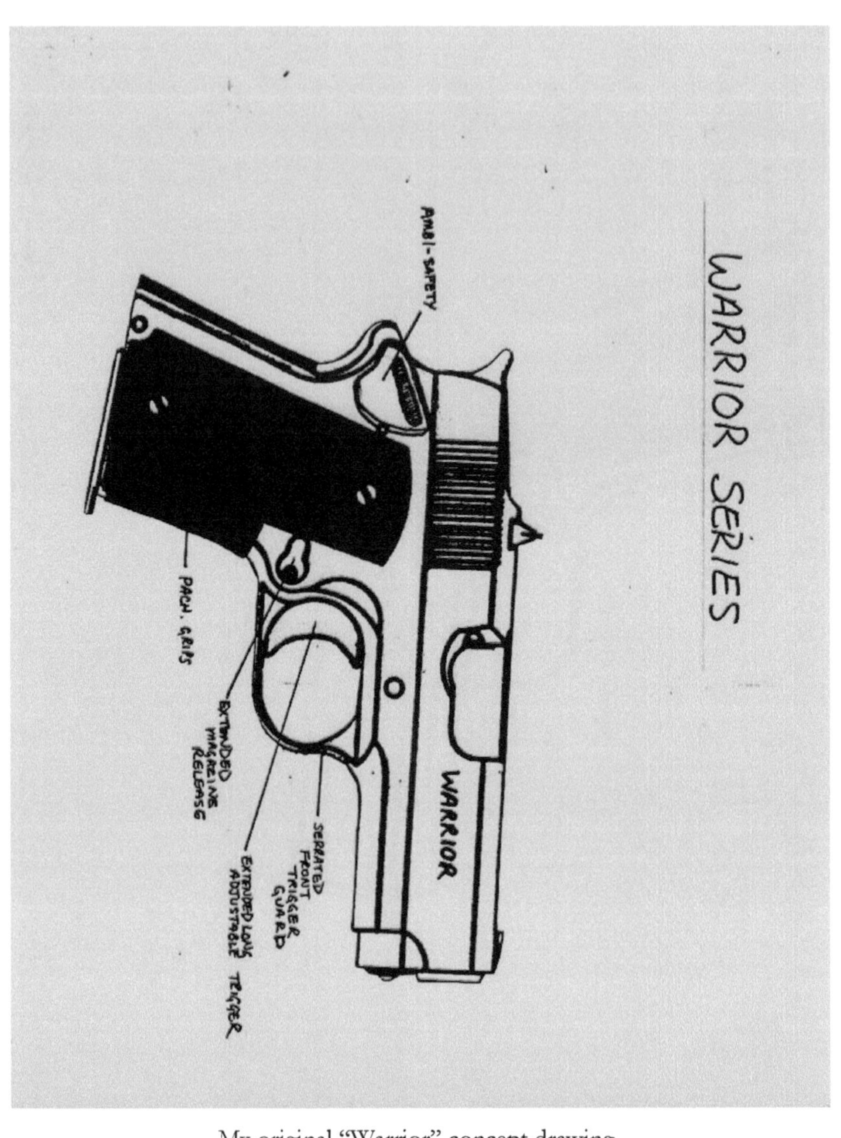

My original "Warrior" concept drawing

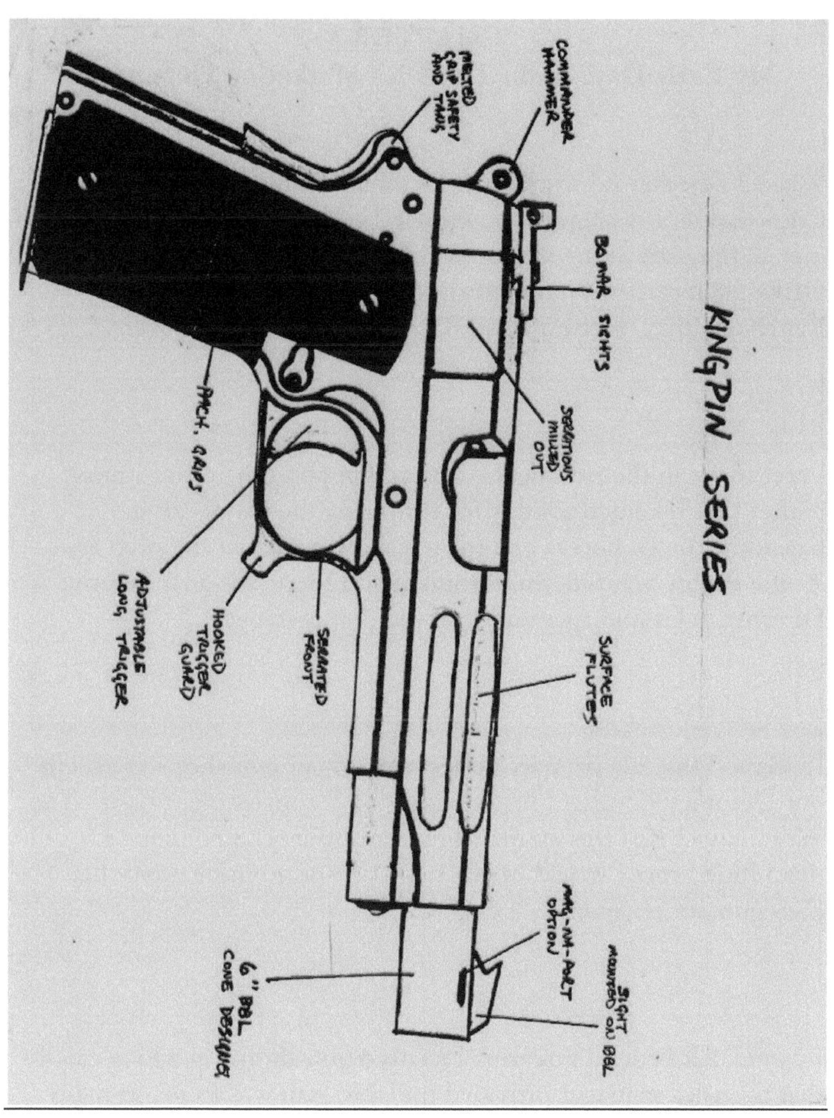

My original "Kingpin" concept drawing

CHAPTER 3

My Early Days in the Detonics Marketing Department

When I first started working at Detonics Manufacturing Corporation, I was given the title of Technical Representative. I met all the staff in my section which included Karen Lowe the Office Manager and Jan Herriott the Customer Service Representative. Her husband Ray was one of the engineers.

I met those in the production line and in gun repair, the ammo crafter that reloaded rounds for test firing the pistols after assembly, the engineers and the guys downstairs in the prep area. At the facility was Sid, the President and there was an Executive Director, sales manager and a production manager.

It seemed that my primary duties were to get gun shops to accept our Detonics Combat Master pistols on a consignment basis. The sales manger had this strategy in place and it seemed that with them hiring me, I would be the main person to implement this consignment program.

I would call Federal Firearms Licensed gun shops on a long call list that the sales manager provided me. My goal was to get as many gun shops as possible to accept six of the Detonics Combat Master pistols on consignment.

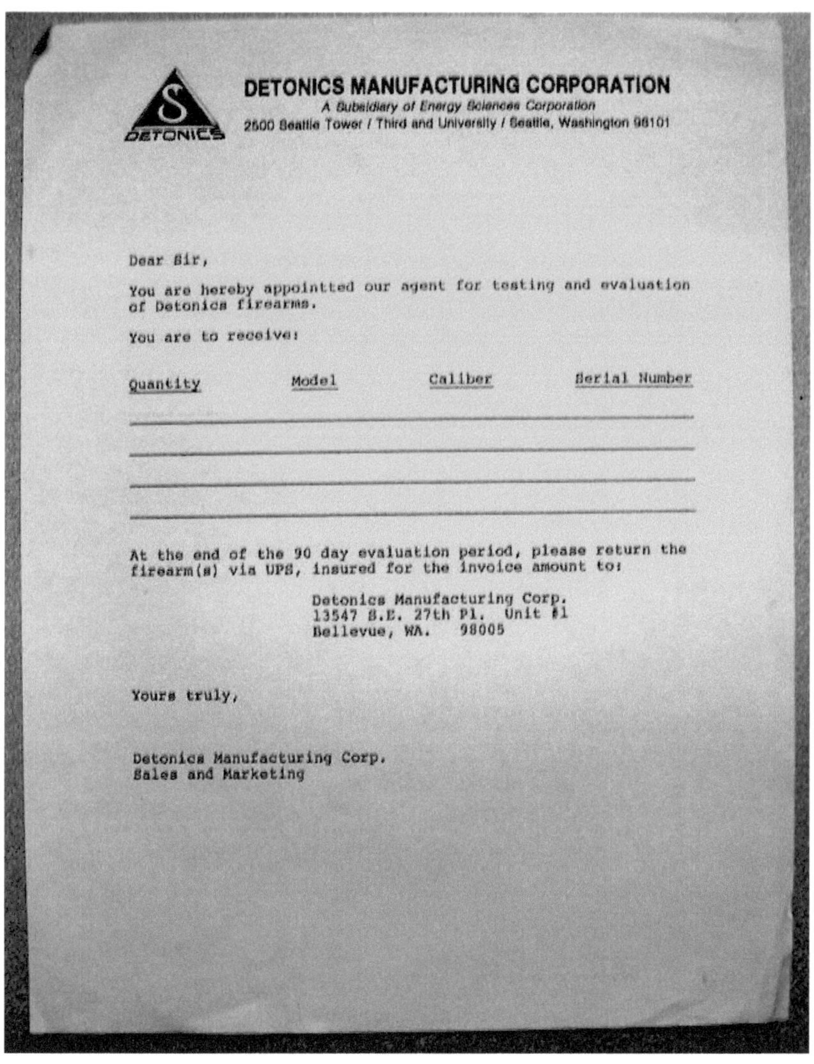

DETONICS MANUFACTURING CORPORATION
A Subsidiary of Energy Sciences Corporation
2500 Seattle Tower / Third and University / Seattle, Washington 98101

Dear Sir,

You are hereby appointted our agent for testing and evaluation of Detonics firearms.

You are to receive:

Quantity	Model	Caliber	Serial Number

At the end of the 90 day evaluation period, please return the firearm(s) via UPS, insured for the invoice amount to:

Detonics Manufacturing Corp.
13547 S.E. 27th Pl. Unit #1
Bellevue, WA. 98005

Yours truly,

Detonics Manufacturing Corp.
Sales and Marketing

The testing and evaluation agreement

My duties included answering correspondence from customers out in the field. This was a time before e-mails. Sometimes the letters were inquires about our products. Other times they were letters complimenting our products for their quality and effectiveness.

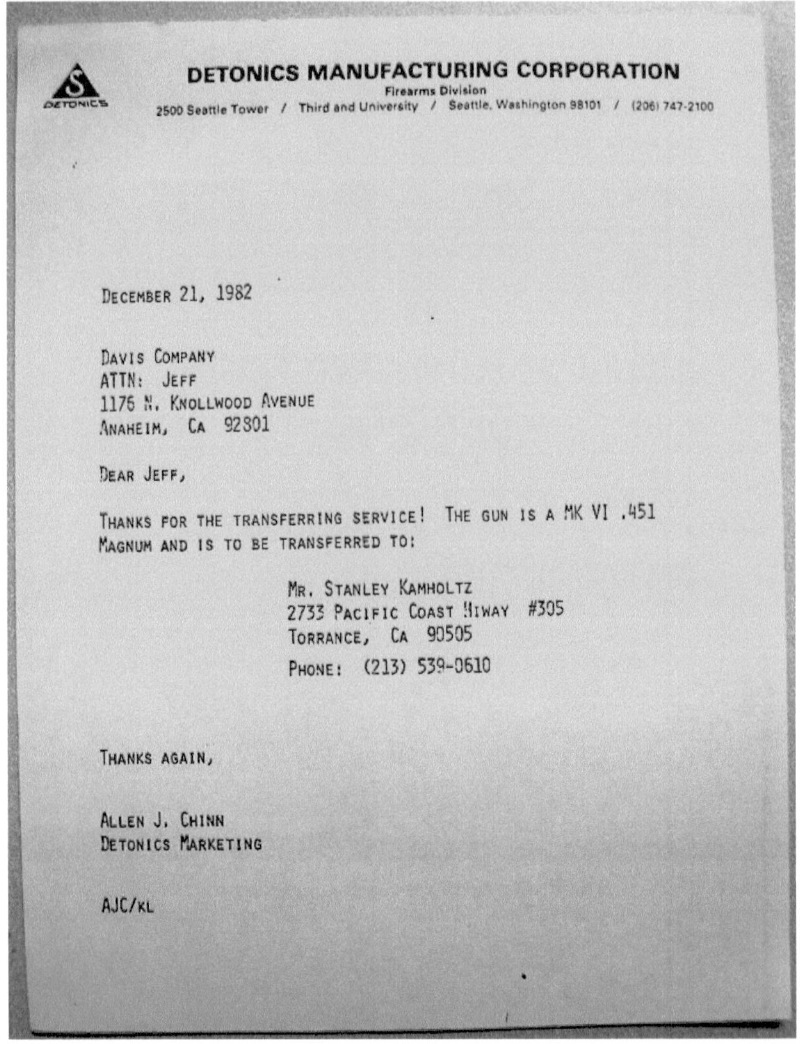

DETONICS MANUFACTURING CORPORATION
Firearms Division
2500 Seattle Tower / Third and University / Seattle, Washington 98101 / (206) 747-2100

DECEMBER 21, 1982

DAVIS COMPANY
ATTN: JEFF
1176 N. KNOLLWOOD AVENUE
ANAHEIM, CA 92801

DEAR JEFF,

THANKS FOR THE TRANSFERRING SERVICE! THE GUN IS A MK VI .451 MAGNUM AND IS TO BE TRANSFERRED TO:

MR. STANLEY KAMHOLTZ
2733 PACIFIC COAST HIWAY #305
TORRANCE, CA 90505
PHONE: (213) 539-0610

THANKS AGAIN,

ALLEN J. CHINN
DETONICS MARKETING

AJC/KL

DETONICS MANUFACTURING CORPORATION

A subsidiary of Energy Sciences Corporation

February 24, 1983

Mr. Steve Fjestad
I.R.I.
1 Apple 3 Square
Minneapolis, MN 55420

Dear Mr. Fjestad:

Mr. Allen Chinn of our Sales & Marketing Dept. has asked me to forward you some information on our guns, including those models which have been discontinued. I will also supply you with information on our .451 Magnum which, because of its limited production, will also have exceptional value in the collector's market.

First of all, the models which have been discontinued:

MK I Matte Blue .45 ACP: Discontinued in December of 1981

MK IV Polished Blue .45 ACP: Discontinued in December of 1981

MK II Satin Nickel .45 ACP: Discontinued in October of 1979

MK III Hard Chrome .45 ACP: Discontinued in October of 1979

* Hard Chrome MK III was produced in very small numbers. Probably no more than twenty (20) MK III's were ever shipped from our factory.

Our .451 Detonics Magnum, which is available in both the MK VI and MK VII configurations, is being produced in a limited quantity. That is to say that we will only produce 1000 .451's and they will be numbered consecutively 1 of 1000 etc.. Because of this limited production, the engraved numbering, and because of the awesome power of this weapon in a very small package, we expect that the value of this gun will increase rapidly in a relatively short time.

Enclosed for your information you will find our current retail price list along with our 1983 catalog which covers our complete product line. If you have any questions or are in need of further information, please feel free to contact me.

Thank-you for your interest in Detonics Manufacturing Corporation and its products.

Very truly yours,

Janet M. Herriott

Janet M. Herriott, Customer Service

2500 Seattle Tower/3rd & University/Seattle, WA 98101/(206) 747-2100

I might add that this was a time period before computers were used in everyday business. All memos were typed on typewriters.

My coworkers found out that my every day carry pistol was a customized Star PD 45 ACP. I had round butted the frame, did a trigger job and glass beaded the frame to a silver color. They gave me a little crap for this, as we worked for Detonics Manufacturing Corporation and we produced the best compact 45 ACP pistol.

Part of my hiring agreement was a "kit gun." I did not know what a "kit gun" was. The guys told me that it was a complete pistol in parts. It would need to be built by one of the gunsmiths.

The gunsmiths included Peter Dunn, Chuck McGough, Richard Niemer, Raul Bloom and Scotty Meeker. Between these five gunsmiths they were the production and repair departments.

I had to approach one of the gunsmiths I met recently and request that they would build a "kit gun" for me. They all seemed to be nice people. I ended up asking Peter Dunn.

Peter was the main person when it came to making pistols run. All the guys were talented, but Peter got to work on most of the critical jobs. He worked on movie director Stanley Kubrick's Detonics Combat Master. All the special pistols and those needing extra attention, ended up on Peter's bench. Peter was always proud of his "Peter Built" (making a pun from the Peterbilt trucks) pistols.

Peter Dunn working at the bench at the original Bellevue facility in 1980

My "Peter Built" Detonics Combat Master was a little different. The pistol was built with a MK V glass beaded surface. The glass beading helped to work harden the surface and reduce glare. The top of the slide had the MC-1 sand blasted surface which further reduced possible glare.

The sights were of the MK VI variety. It had the blades of various heights for adjustment for height of impact. There were no marking on the pistol other than the factory stamp and the serial number. Pachmayr grips and a flat mainspring housing completed this great pistol. Peter did an outstanding job and the trigger was crisp and clean.

"Peter Built" Detonics Combat Master

My custom Detonics Combat Master was indeed a fine fighting tool. It was very accurate and outstandingly reliable. My favorite load was the Speer 200 grain jacketed hollow point. This was a bullet with a hollow point larger than half the diameter of the bullet. Nicknamed the "flying ashtray" this was usually the hardest of the hollow point bullets to make feed reliably in 45 ACP autos. My "Peter Built" fed these with utter reliability. This pistol would be my constant companion for many years to come.

"Peter Built" Detonics Combat Master with slide locked back

Working each day at the factory, coworkers would talk about Sid. Everyone knew a little bit of Sid's background. He had many stories and yet he was still shrouded in mystery.

Amongst the rules at the factory, one was very important. No one was permitted to carry a loaded pistol except for Sid and Marc Logan, the Production Manager.

Marc one day mentioned this policy to me. He was the Production Manager and was Sergeant at Arms. This gave him the responsibility to safeguard the facility, hence the ability to carry a loaded handgun.

He then mentioned a situation once when Sid was either bored, or decided to give the guys in production a heart attack. He said that Sid checked out one of the Combat Masters built to fire the 9mm blanks. Marc said that Sid walked in and started "hosing" everyone. The 9mm blanks were loud and almost gave everyone heart failure and brown shorts!

Marc then mentioned another incident where the ammo crafter had the radio too loud. He was told to turn it down, but it soon went back up in volume. After a couple of times Sid had enough. He calmly walked over to the radio and shot it with one of his "elevator loads." It was essentially a 308 case that was shortened and formed to hold a buckshot pellet to cover a birdshot load underneath. The radio was destroyed and that was the end of that.

The stages to make 45 ACP shotshells or "elevator loads"

Marc knew that I was a Kung-Fu instructor and mentioned that he was one of Sid's students. He mentioned that Sid's skills were amazing and that his he also had mental powers as well. I asked what he meant by that and he stated that Sid had the power to "throw" green snakes at you with his mind. He explained that Sid had done that to him and he visualized green snakes being thrown at him.

One day Sid was discussing gunfighting techniques at the front office. I walked in and became a part of the listening group. Sid mentioned how to engage an opponent coming from the right side. He demonstrated a quick snap shooting method that had the pistol in a horizontal position. Funny that we make fun of the horizontal "gangster" pistol hold, but this was very similar to this. It was just done in a quick, aggressive snap shooting action.

Sid then asked the group "Do you know what to do if your opponent comes up from behind you and has the drop on you?" No one responded. Sid then quickly dropped his upper body and shot backwards between his legs. He mentioned that there weren't too many options, but if you were lucky, the opponent would be aiming at your head. "Dropping down quickly and shooting backwards between your legs may be the only chance you get." he said.

As usual, Sid had everyone's attention and everyone was mesmerized.

Detonics Manufacturing Corporation had many products and learning about them was easy and I had a keen interest. I was in heaven!

Colored circular from the early 1980s

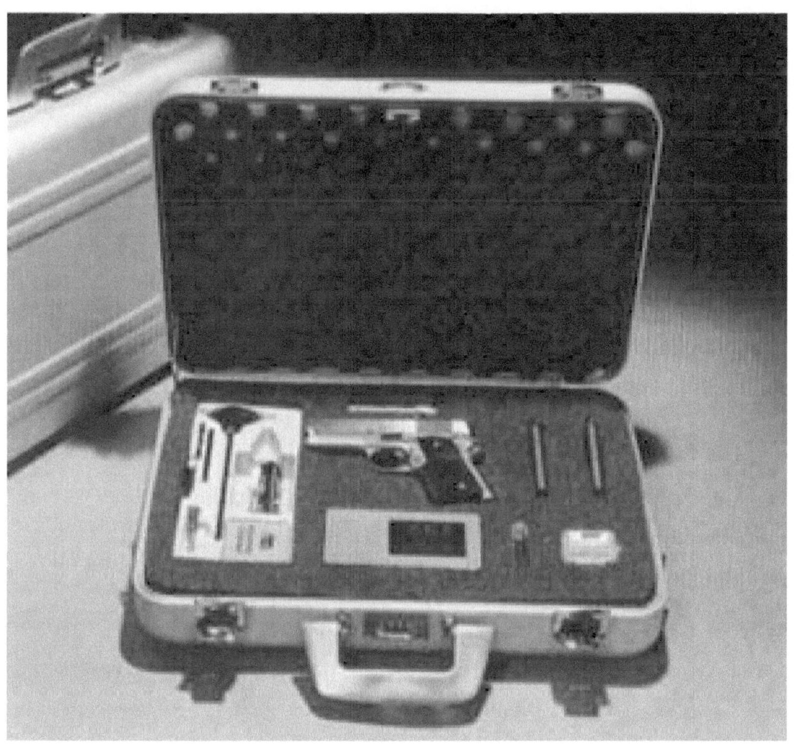

Combat Master 45 ACP / 451 Detonics Mag set in Halliburton case

Factory picture of Combat Masters MK V, MK VI and MK VII

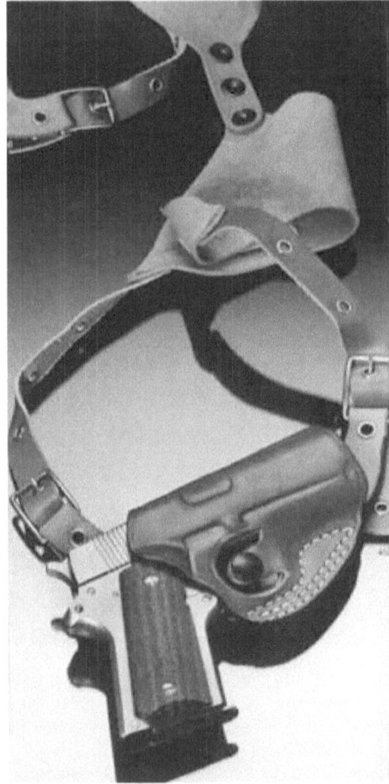

Alessi Leather provided holsters for Detonics Manufacturing Corporation

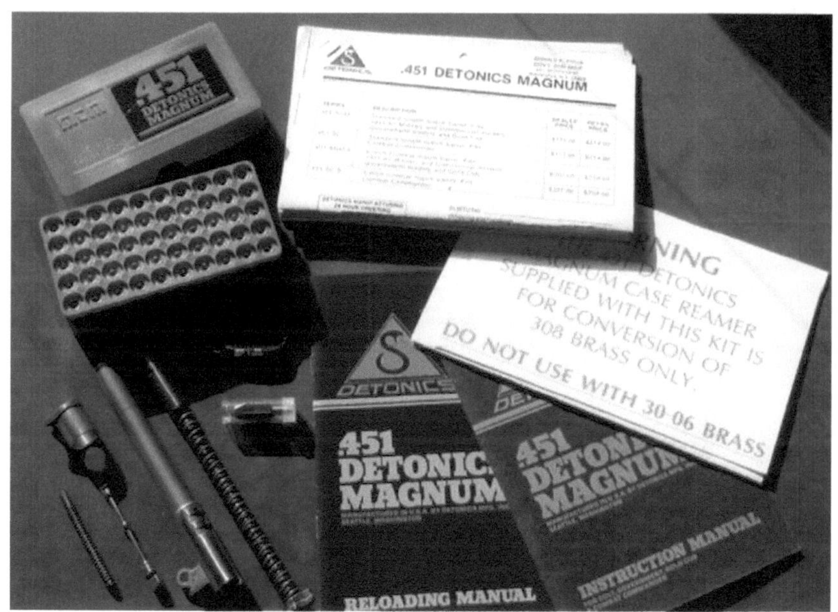

451 Detonics Magnum Conversion Kit

Combat Master Field Stripped

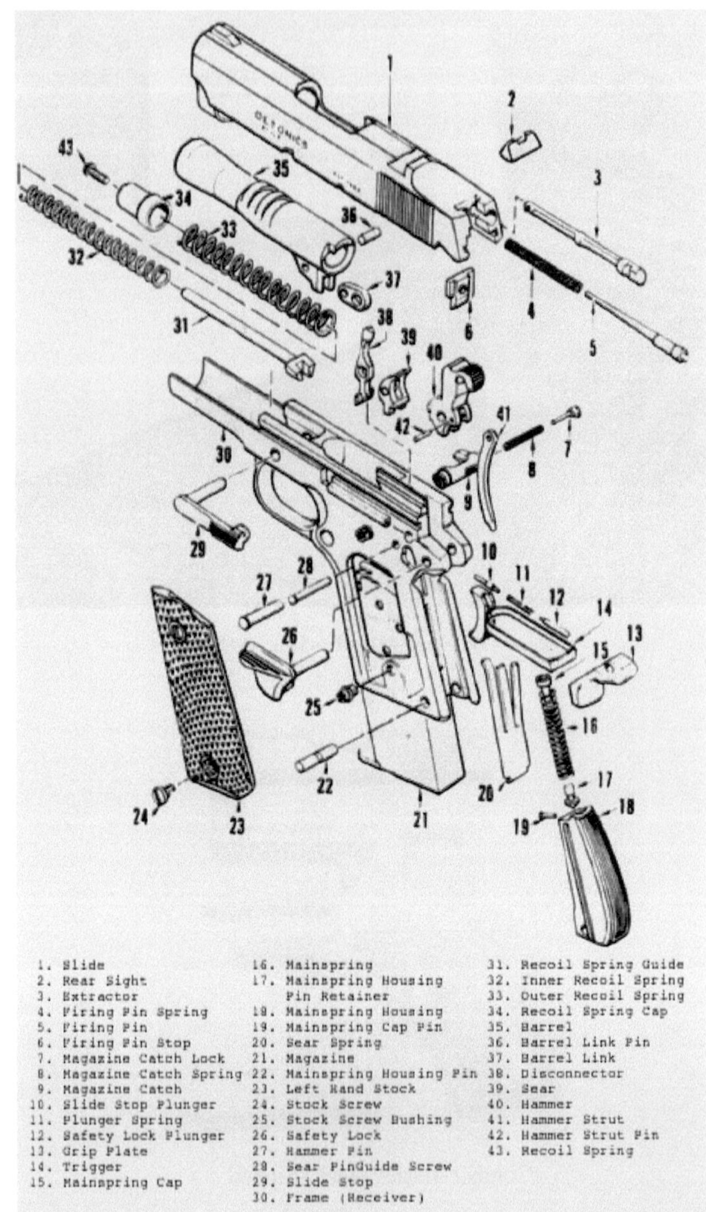
1. Slide
2. Rear Sight
3. Extractor
4. Firing Pin Spring
5. Firing Pin
6. Firing Pin Stop
7. Magazine Catch Lock
8. Magazine Catch Spring
9. Magazine Catch
10. Slide Stop Plunger
11. Plunger Spring
12. Safety Lock Plunger
13. Grip Plate
14. Trigger
15. Mainspring Cap
16. Mainspring
17. Mainspring Housing Pin Retainer
18. Mainspring Housing
19. Mainspring Cap Pin
20. Sear Spring
21. Magazine
22. Mainspring Housing Pin
23. Left Hand Stock
24. Stock Screw
25. Stock Screw Bushing
26. Safety Lock
27. Hammer Pin
28. Sear PinGuide Screw
29. Slide Stop
30. Frame (Receiver)
31. Recoil Spring Guide
32. Inner Recoil Spring
33. Outer Recoil Spring
34. Recoil Spring Cap
35. Barrel
36. Barrel Link Pin
37. Barrel Link
38. Disconnector
39. Sear
40. Hammer
41. Hammer Strut
42. Hammer Strut Pin
43. Recoil Spring

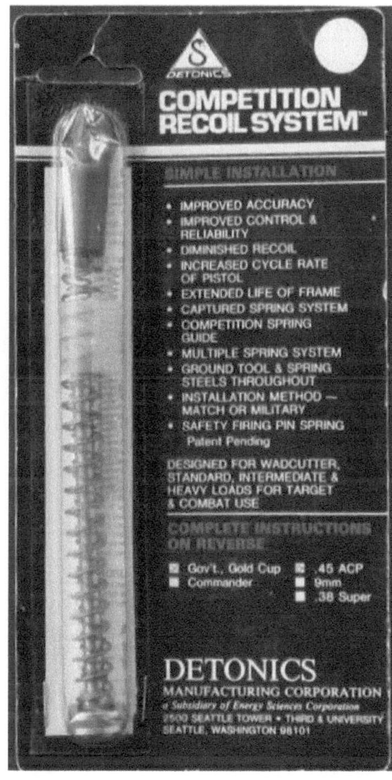

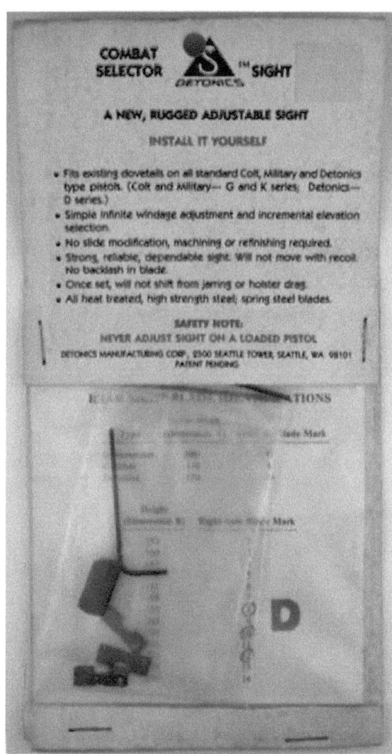

Competition Recoil System and Combat Master MK VI Sight (top row)
Detonics Pewter Belt Buckle and Detonics Sticker (bottom row)

CHAPTER 4
Sid's Stories

I soon found myself like a school boy. I loved hearing about his exploits and found myself finishing my sales and marketing duties as soon as possible so I could visit Sid in his office.

Sid in his office at the original Bellevue facility

Sid was always so nice, friendly and informative. Most of the informative stories he gave me were in bits and pieces. No dates or locations were ever discussed.

One day we were talking about martial arts and he said, "Do you know how I started in martial arts?" I responded "No." Then Sid continued, "I had a friend in high school. He told me to go down to the dojo and that his father was the instructor. I went down there and walked through the door. Of course I had my shoes on and before I could say what I was there for they threw me out into the street. I picked myself up and went back into the dojo. They grabbed me and threw me out again. I went in a third time and they grabbed me again, but as they were about to throw me out, my friend stopped them and said I was with him. And that is how I started in the martial arts."

Another time Sid mentioned that he was recruited into the OSS (Office of Strategic Services) because he was used to shooting, hunting and blowing up stuff. This organization was the United States equivalent of the British Secret Intelligence Service. This World War II agency was the forerunner to the CIA (Central Intelligence Agency).

Army photo months prior to entry into the Office of Strategic Services

Sid mentioned that during the Second World War, he spent three years learning at Shaolin Temple. He mentioned that some of the monks had the ability to use their minds. Some could "throw" snakes at their opponents. He said some monks had the specialized technique to eat certain herbs to create a horrid, vile, stench coming from their breath. This would distract their opponents to the point they would almost vomit.

He said one time a monk brought him out to a fenced chicken area. Sid said, "Not speaking English, the monk pointed at me and then at a chicken. I pointed at myself and then at a chicken and the monk nodded his head. I pointed at a chicken, and then the monk pointed at the chicken. It jumped up, flapping its wings and dropped dead, bleeding from its eyes and ears. The monk wanted me to pick out two more. I did and the same results happened."

Sometime after World War II, Sid trained at the Kodokan in Japan and received his black belt there. He mentioned that he was approached with the offer of secret training that would increase his martial arts abilities and power. He agreed to do so. Sid went to the building that was at a secret location. There he was met by security staff and paid his fee.

He was then escorted to another hallway and a guard let them through. Sid and his escort went down another hallway and was admitted by another guard and directed to go to another hallway. They went through two more check points and finally Sid was permitted to enter the hall that would be where this secret training would take place.

As Sid entered the large hall, he was surprised. All he saw was a large number of men chasing naked young women! "This was the secret martial arts training to increase power and skills!" Sid said with a slight smile as he peered over his glasses.

Sid told me, "I once had a Chinese bodyguard. He was pretty good. We were in a bar in South America. Suddenly my bodyguard opened fire with his Uzi at the other end of the bar. We asked him why he shot the man and the bodyguard said he was going for a gun. We kicked the dead body over and his right hand was going for a pistol."

Sid continued and said, "Another time we were in another bar and the same situation happened. My bodyguard opened fire with his Uzi and a man dropped dead at the end of the bar. When we kicked over the dead body, this man was going for a pack of cigarettes."

Sid said sometimes you can't avoid civilian casualties. He mentioned, "One time we just stepped out of a building. The evening was just starting to get dark. At the end of the street a large, dark sedan started up its engine. They didn't turn on their lights and started speeding down the street towards us. We thought it was a "hit" and my bodyguard opened fire and emptied his Uzi into the speeding car. The car crashed at the end of the street. Unfortunately, we found five nuns. They were late for a meeting and forgot to turn on their headlights."

One time Sid told me about a story that involved a Mafia informant. He said, "Two guys were taken by Mafia members to a warehouse. They didn't know which one was the informant, so they nailed both of them to the wooden floor. The large nails went through the fleshy part of their arms and legs. One of the guys took a dull ax and started by chopping off at the ankle. Then the other ankle went. He kept chopping six inch sections of his legs off. By the time he got to the knees, the other person admitted that he was the informant and started screaming that he would tell them everything.

At that time three federal agents and the local police did a house cleaning to save the informant. All of the Mafia members were killed by the three federal agents. We couldn't save the one person that was chopped up. He died from shock and blood loss."

Sid told me, "I was once called in on a case that was peculiar and had the local police baffled. It seemed that several senior men were dying in this small town. We figured out the unusual cause of these deaths. It appeared that one senior woman had made her husband some fish for lunch, but he ran late. When he got home later that afternoon, the fish had been sitting out for hours, but he ate it anyway. He felt ill later and eventually died. No one thought anything about this situation as he was an old man.

A short time later friends of the senior woman asked what happened and what got her husband ill. She told her friends that all she did was make fish for his lunch and it was left out for hours until he finally got back home. All of a sudden one of her friends tried this and her husband died and then another one did it too. We figured out the pattern and the fact that all the husbands had died from botulism."

Sid one day said, "You know why I came up with the idea for the Detonics? On some missions I had to carry two 45s. I wanted to have something easier to conceal and have totally reliability. That is why I came up with it."

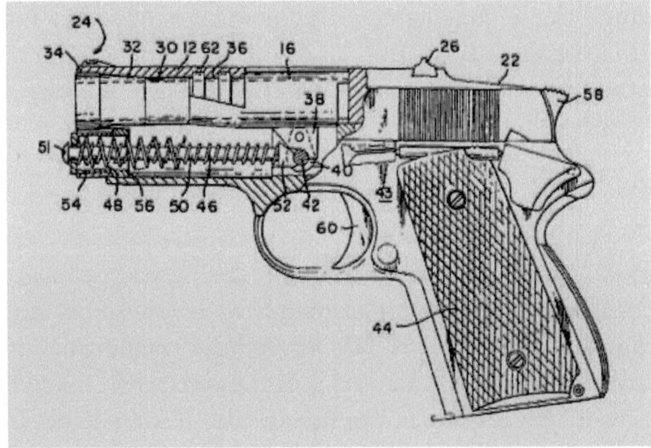

Back in 1983 there was a Kabar knife on Sid's office wall. In the shadow box that contained the knife there was a little note that simply said, "To Sid. From the boys." I asked Sid about it and he mentioned that one of the members of his former OSS unit showed a picture of them on national television. He said that "the boys" went to his office and took the Kabar off his wall as a message not to parade pictures that could identify the old OSS operatives.

I put "two and two together" and remembered seeing the ABC 20/20 telecast. The subject of the report was Mitch Werbell and his mercenary school "The Farm" in Georgia. I remembered seeing the show and the black and white picture of the OSS operatives. The show stated that in the picture were the current (in 1983) CIA Director, William J. Casey and Mitch Werbell. Sid was in that picture! Sid later confirmed that this was the very picture that got him and CIA Director, William J. Casey upset.

Sid told me that some of his jobs required infiltrating a facility to ensure they had property security. Sid told me, "Once I had to break into a heavily secured facility on the East Coast. It was secured with monitors, barbed wire, fencing, electronic sensors and a large security team inside the facility. There was no way to get passed all the monitors, barbed wire, fencing and electronic sensors. They would catch a team of people trying to get passed any one of those security measures. So I waited.

I waited long enough to wait for the next rain storm. When it occurred I had some men set the electronic sensors off, but hid and was not noticed. The next time the heavy rains came, we did the same thing. Another rain storm came and my men set the electronic sensors off again, but were not caught. I basically conditioned the security team of the facility to believe that every time the heavy rains came, the electronic sensors would send out false alarms.

We then went in at the next rain storm. My team of men crossed the area with the electronic sensors. The security team believing the alarm was false was caught totally off guard."

Then Sid gave another example, "Once on the West Coast there was a facility that I was supposed to break their security. They had a heavily armed security team and the front gate had a guard. Inside they had monitors to watch the front gate.

We were close to Hollywood, so I found some pretty girls and hired them to be a distraction. I had two of the girls were near the front gate and all of a sudden started arguing. They were off to the side and the arguing turned into a fight. The guard ran over trying to stop the fight. Then the girls started to tear each other's clothes off. Well, all the guys watching the monitors inside the facility had their eyes glued on all the action. Soon other guys went to watch the monitors too. Then I had a third girl jump in the fight.

With all this going on and with all the guys distracted watching half naked women fighting, my team drove in and took over the facility."

Sid supervising a friend firing an Uzi submachine gun

CHAPTER 5
Tidbits from Sid

Sid would always have little amazing comments or short stories about things or items.

I remember asking him if he ever used a "hush puppy." A "hush puppy" was a very effective silencer used to "hush" sentry dogs, hence the term "hush puppy." He replied yes. He remembered that he was in a hotel and was waiting to do a job. He said he had stacked a bunch of telephone books and practiced one afternoon. He shot a brick of 22s and no one noticed. A brick of 22s was 500 rounds of 22 long rifle ammunition.

One time Sid asked me if I knew what nicotine sulfate was. He then told me that it was a very highly toxic poison. He said that they would mix it with DMSO and the mixture would penetrate the skin very easily. They would put the deadly combination in a felt marker. When needed all you would have to do is take the cap off a take a swipe across the target's neck and they would go down.

Sid asked me if I knew what a shape charge was. I replied no. He explained that a shape charge was an explosive charge designed to focus the effect of the explosive's energy. He said they were very useful and that there were many types of shape charges. Sid stated, "One type of shape charge was very tiny, about the size of a fifty cent piece. It had Velcro on the back. A person could bump into you on the street, apologize and then pat you "innocently" on the back. You would walk away with a miniature shape charge until it was detonated."

Early in our friendship we would go out for a dark beer, or out to lunch. Sid was always careful to pick a seat with a wall behind him and a good view of the people and things in front of him. He would find a seat that he liked and asked "You don't mind if I sit here do you?" I would smile and shake my head no.

Sid told me about getting impromptu practice in the Pioneer Square area by having a few bills hanging out of his pockets. He said it would be good practice as you would never know exactly what they would do. Sometimes he said he would dress "down" to look the part of someone that actually might frequent the area.

One day in Sid's office he showed me a pen gun. This was an incredible little weapon that fired a 22 rimfire cartridge. It looked very much like a regular pen, but in special circumstances it would provide the agent a weapon that would propel a small lead bullet into an opponent.

One day Sid was walking towards his office and saw me in the production area. He stopped over and said, "You see this? See if you can hold it perfectly still." I tried, but the little tiny silver colored switch moved. And it continued to move. Sid then said, "You can't hold it still. The switch will move no matter how still you try to hold it. Even your heartbeat will magnify the movement of the switch until the detonator goes boom." He finished with a sly, little smile and turned walking in to his office.

Once Sid had the sales manager followed. The sale manager was doing a sales trip and was down South. Sid received the detailed report from one of the operatives he knew that was "just keeping in practice." I remembered the sales manager and Sid laughed as they discussed the situation. Sid made a few references to where the sale manager had gone and they both thought it was funny.

At Detonics we were discussing various calibers one day and I believe we mentioned the Pocket Nine and Sid commented, "A 9mm lacks power. It may be good for a woman to carry." Of course Sid always carried his Combat Master in 45 ACP.

For one of the public offerings we were all coming up with ideas that Energy Sciences / Detonics Manufacturing Corporation could possibly produce. Sid came up with the fact that in the 1800s the French had developed an air rifle that shot a .50 caliber lead ball and was capable of killing deer at 100 yards. Sid said that the stock would hold the air reservoir.

Parts of Sid's research lead him to buy a Benjamin 22 caliber air rifle. He had a metal button that he tied with a short length of string and suspended it in the ceiling in the corner of the production room. When he was bored he would occasionally shoot at the hanging button from his office chair. He would also sometimes shoot out of his office window. Across the parking lot was the company's CNC machine building. He would shoot at the cement posts in front of the entry doors. Sid was the President of the company. Quoting a line from a Mel Brooks movie, "It's good to be the king!"

In 1983 Sid came down to my Bellevue Kung-Fu Club and demonstrated to my students. He demonstrated self defense with joint locking and defense against an attacker with a club. Sid was fluid and very effective.

Between working at Detonics and running my Bellevue Kung-Fu Club I was quite busy. One evening a Bellevue Fire Fighter stopped over to the school and asked if I ever did any bodyguard or security escort work. I replied that I had not, but this individual was still interested in having me escort he and his business partner to Paraguay. He stated that they had developed an assault rifle and the tooling could be used to make pots and pans also. They were supposed to meet in Paraguay in a few weeks and offered a fairly good sum of money for me to be their bodyguard. I mentioned this to a couple of the gunsmiths at Detonics. Hearing this, Sid immediately stopped by my Kung-Fu school. With a smile and "enlarged eyes" he said, "I heard you were thinking about being a

BG. Don't! The BG always gets it first!" I knew Sid was right and with that I contacted the would-be clients and declined the offer.

I had told Sid I would go to his Green Lake class and demonstrate. This was still in 1983. I first got lost and ended up at the Green Lake Wing Chun Kung-Fu School. I was redirected and finally made it to Sid's class. It was at this demonstration of traditional Kung-Fu skills that Sid tested my skill. It was a very minor test, but a test none the less. After demonstrating striking, kicking, steel whip and saber, Sid addressed his students and stated that one must be proficient with a weapon like it was an extension of our bodies. I was holding my saber when he stepped forward to me striking at my head. I quickly blocked the upper attack. Immediately he did a surprise upward attack to my mid section. I instinctively blocked by quickly dropping the saber to meet the upward bound stick. I successfully passed Sid's test of my reflexes and if my techniques were part of my spirit.

I was sitting in Sid's office one afternoon. His phone rang and he ended up with discussing military equipment and troops. He said over phone that there should be x number of armored cars with self-inflating tires, x number of troops should be available and x number of jets should be on call. He mentioned other items as well. I asked Sid who was that on the phone. He calmly said, "I was answering security questions for the protection of the South Korean President."

I was having problems with the sales manager. It appeared that the sales manager started to get jealous of my relationship with Sid and was making things difficult for me. One day Sid pulled me to the side and said with a smile, "Don't worry about him. We both know we can outshoot him, outfight him, and out fuck him!" I smiled and Sid got me to be less stressed about the incompetent sales manager.

Sid gave me two gifts that tasted blood. He knew that I could appreciate a "real" weapon that had tasted blood in actual battle.

The first weapon was a pair of sai. These well worn sai were used by a hit man. This iron weapon was used to create heavy side impact or deadly forward penetration with the shaft. The killer's trademark was to drive the cone shaped butt of the handle through his victim's eye socket. Sid followed him all over Asia and finally tracking down this person in a dark alley. When the hit man pulled out the sai ready to attack, Sid quickly dispatched the killer with his 1911 pistol.

The second one was a French style machete. It was very heavy duty and was accompanied with a leather sheath. Sid smiled and said, "I know that you would appreciate this. It was used in Burma in the 1950s. It had taken a head or two."

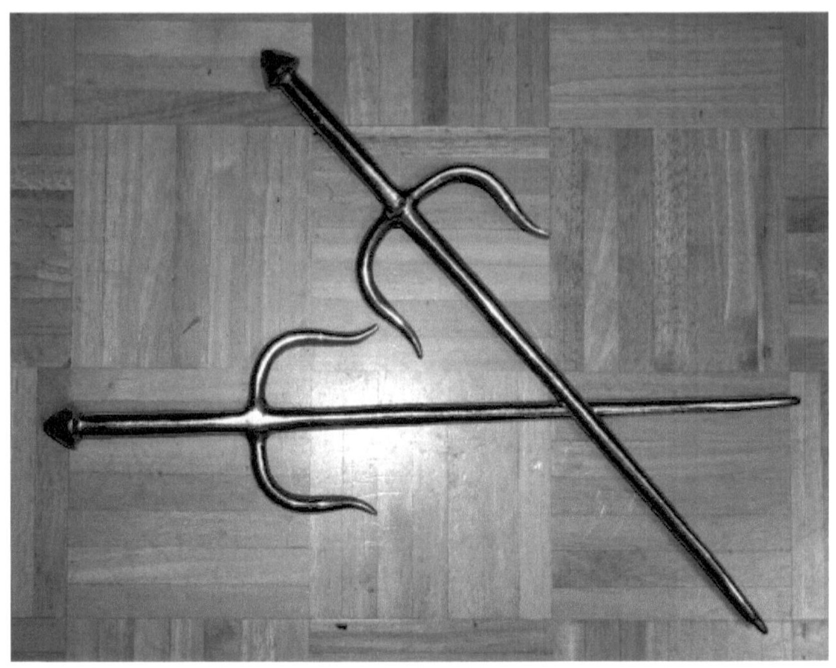

Hit man's sai captured by Sid

Sid's French style machete used in Burma in the 1950s

After my departure from Detonics Manufacturing Corporation, I was very busy with being a Parks and Recreation Professional for the City of Seattle. I lost track of Sid, as I was trying to keep my head above water at work and I was raising two boys.

We were destined to meet again and I found him as we were both demonstrating at the 1994 Northwest Martial Arts Expo in Seattle's Chinatown.

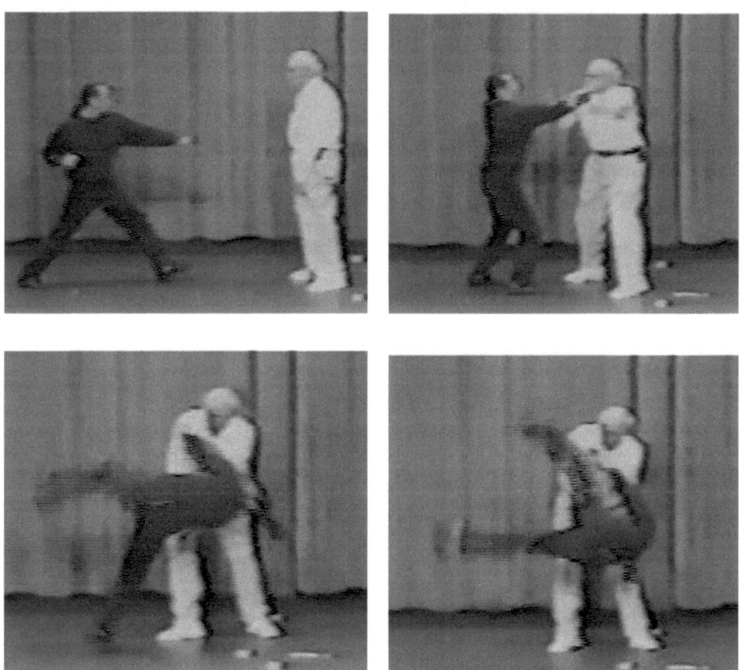

Sid demonstrating defense against a roundhouse punch. As the attacker's punch approaches, Sid steps forward and intercepts the right arm. Sid then steps back with his left leg and executes an elbow throw.

Sid demonstrating defense against an overhead knife attack. As the attacker's knife is coming downward, Sid steps to his left and assists the knife to continue its circular path. The knife is buried into the attacker's stomach.

Sid defending against a wrist grab. As the attacker grabs Sid's left wrist, Sid steps back with his left foot and at the same time he places his right hand on the exposed neck. Sid flows with the attacker's momentum, slamming him to the ground. Sid then follows up with a downward punch to the attacker's mid section.

Sid defending against a pistol pointed at his back. Sid notices the pistol with a quick visual check. His right leg steps back as he shoots his right arm back, deflecting the weapon away from his body. Sid then quickly reaches up and locks his two hands and applies downwards pressure to the attacker's elbow. This drives the attacker violently down to the ground.

Sid demonstrating how not to defend against a pistol pointed at your back. Sid places his finger against the defender's back and holds the pistol back in a safe position. The defender without doing a visual check starts to go into the defensive technique with the step and arm deflect. Sid shoots the defender down.

For many years I had been doing large martial arts exhibitions while I was working for the City of Seattle. I had taken a couple of years off from doing the event and past participants decided to do one for a fundraiser to send their school to a national competition.

Sid demonstrating Kiai Jitsu. Self defense using his voice and his mind.

Sid did an outstanding demonstration of joint locking and self defense. He successfully defended against grabs, punches, knife, bat, pistol and even a samurai sword. Sid also demonstrated self defense with his mind and voice. The art was called Kiai Jitsu. I resumed my annual martial arts exhibitions and was proud to have Sid perform the following year.

When I wrote my first book "A Kung-Fu Master's Journey" I stated that Sid was amongst my closest martial arts friends. I wrote down the following:

Sid had an extensive background in Aiki-Jujitsu. He possessed a black belt from the Kodokan in Japan. He also studied Shaolin Kung-Fu for several years while behind enemy lines during World War II. He was also a Karateka.

Grandmaster Woodcock's Accomplishments:

Grandmaster, 3rd Style Shaolin Kung-Fu

8th Degree Black Belt in Shinobi

Instructor, U.S. Army Special Forces, Ft. Bragg

Instructor, U.S. Navy Seal Teams

Consultant, U.S. Department of Defense

Consultant, Federal Bureau of Investigation

Consultant, Central Intelligence Agency

Consultant, U.S. Secret Service

Director and Federal Liaison for Special Warfare, in the areas of counter terrorist training.

I'm sure that there was so much more that he could not include.

At one point in time I was thinking about doing a book on mixed martial arts and asked Sid if he knew William Fairbairn and Rex

Applegate. He said "Yes, I knew Willie." He also confirmed he was friends with Rex Applegate too.

Sid also mentioned that in his collection he had an early leather handled prototype of the Sykes-Fairbairn knife. We both knew this treasure was worth a “king's ransom” as this famous World War II knife was mass produced with a cast metal handle.

Sid was always keeping himself busy. For years he had been teaching his class in Kirkland. He was also teaching self defense to Federal Air Marshals. He would teach hand to hand, disarming techniques and strategies.

Sid had amazing things in his possession. I remember seeing what seemed to be prototype cartridges that were designated with factory head stamps. However, I never heard of some of them. One that caught my eye was a 5.45x45mm. I own 5.45x39mm and 5.56x45mm (223) rifles, but I've never heard of a 5.45x45mm. This fired case had a factory head stamp. This was probably an attempt to mate the Russian 5.45mm bullet with the American 45mm case.

Two years ago I was at the Washington Athletic Club and discussing possible classes and training opportunities I could offer. One of their members Danner Graves brought up Sid's name. He had met Sid once and was so impressed with his self defense techniques. He suggested I offer a men's self-defense class. I stated that I did try to offer one, but the majority of "guys" thought that they are capable and would be "alright." I told Danner and the staff I would be willing to offer one in the future.

After taking Sid to dinner last year, he stated that he had to teach class. Then he asked if I would like to visit his class that evening. I replied that I would. We went to his class in Kirkland and he asked me to lead his class. I demonstrated combat knife techniques and his students followed in a few drills.

I brought Sid a DVD with videos of me performing hand techniques, as well as various weapons. Sid watched and smiled at me. "You still have it old buddy!" he said.

In 2010, I organized a class reunion of my students over the years. Sid hadn't been driving much, but he drove over to Seattle and happily surprised me at the event. As soon as he got there, some of the older students remembered Sid and paid respect to "Sifu Woodcock."

Newer students found themselves engaged and mesmerized with a few short stories. That was just part of Sid's magic.

Grandmasters Sid Woodcock and Allen J. Chinn in 2010

Sid was concerned that the papers from China that verified his rank as a Grandmaster in Chin Na were misplaced in his move to the new apartment down the hall - I said "Don't worry Sid. We know what level you are." He smiled and that seemed to put that one to rest.

CHAPTER 6

Detonics – The Good, Bad and Ugly

Early Detonics' Combat Master pistols were made from carbon steel Essex frames and slides. These were "cut and welds." The original cone was silver soldered in place. The original recoil spring cap was "captured" with the use of a common paper clip. This would help when disassembling the pistol.

Eventually the Combat Master would be made in all stainless steel. Cal Foster (Caspian) castings were later used. Detonics were unique as they were the only all stainless steel pistols that functioned without galling. The AMT Hardballer had problems and some resorted to weird concoctions like grease and STP. Smith and Wesson used hard chromed barrels and sometimes other parts to work around the galling issue.

The Detonics Combat Master with its stainless steel parts hardened to different hardness levels alleviated the galling issue. This creative solution permitted the pistol to function without seizing or galling. A typical light oil film would be all this pistol would require.

Detonics Manufacturing Corporation's Combat Master was indeed a very unique pistol. At the time it was the most compact, concealable, reliable, accurate and powerful handgun in the world. It featured a very large opened and lower ejection port, tuned extractor, highly visible combat sights, shortened grip frame for ease of concealment, shortened barrel and slide to enable the fastest draw, lightened slide for fast cycling and reduced felt recoil and an effective captured recoil system to aid in the fast cycling and ease of disassembling.

It was made in carbon steel with various finishes and finally in the very durable, weather resistant stainless steel. The Combat Master was offered in 45 ACP, 9mm, 38 Super and 451 Detonics.

Sid's pistol concept became a reality. It was everything that he ever imagined. It was an outstanding fighting pistol conceived by fighting man. It had so many custom features and they built it to be mass produced. The expensive price tag of this pistol was nowhere near what one would pay for a customized fighting pistol with all these features.

The Detonics Combat Master was quick to draw, accurate, reliable, hit with power and was easy to conceal. It was fighting pistol not for everyone. It was also misunderstood, as some people have very different ideas on what a fighting pistol (or revolver) should be.

I was busy continuing the sales manager's consignment program. I believe he wanted to get as much product out to the public and hoped that the increased exposure and possibility for sales would be a positive for the company.

Unfortunately these pistols were retailing in the mid and upper four hundred dollar range. Materials and labor had already been paid as production cost for the pistols. The company was also paying shipping to the gun shops. Add shipping cost and advertising and there was quite a bit of money tied up into each of those pistols.

However, money coming in was not coming in as fast as the sales manager had hoped.

I believe the sales manager missed the mark and should have simply marketed the Combat Master as the exclusive pistol built for combat effectiveness. A list of the exclusive features and typical cost by quality gunsmiths could have sold interested individuals on the cost savings by this "custom production" combat pistol. A Colt with custom gunsmithing to match the features of the Combat Master would have been much more than the retail value of our pistol.

Nehemiah Sirkis was a firearms designer for Detonics Manufacturing Corporation. Before working at Detonics Manufacturing he was already a famous firearms designer, had a history with the Israeli military and also represented Israel in the Olympics in precision shooting.

Nehemiah a year earlier had a "bullpup" sniper M-14 design that was under consideration for possible production. The Sirkis M33 sniper rifle was evidence that at times Detonics Manufacturing Corporation was indeed bold, creative and innovative.

August 11, 1982

Memo to: Mike Maes

cc: Sid Woodcock
Ray Herriott

Subject: Sirkis M33 Combat Sniper Weapon System (otherwise Nehemia's Sniper Rifle) or ... the 10 - ring Sirkis (per Paul)

1) Nehemia's Sniper Rifle (described in detail in the attached) is a semi-automatic rifle, based on the M-14 action with a "bull-pup" stock and detachable scope mount.

2) The M-14 already enjoys an excellent reputation for accuracy and Nehemia's modifications, including a full floating barrel (a barrel attached only to the action, not to the stock) should make it a real "tack-driver." Nehemia's goal is minute of angle accuracy (1" in 100 yards) and I see no reason why this can not be achieved.

3) The M-14 action was developed by John Garand and others at Springfield Armory for the U.S. Government. Even if patented at the time, the patents would have now expired since the M-14 hasn't been made since 1963. M-14 lookalikes are currently made by the commercial firm "Springfield Armory" and we should have no problem in obtaining actions.

4) As designed, incorporating the Bull-pup stock and M-14 action, Nehemia's rifle cannot be fired from the left shoulder. There are no "left-hand" M-14 actions available as there is no need for such a modification to an automatic rifle in normal use. The M-14, like all Garand rifles, ejects up and forward to the right.

In considering the lack of ambidextrous capability in what is basically a military weapon, the following points should be considered;

- None of the military bolt actions in use up through World War II (Springfield, Lee-Enfield, Mauser, Mosin-Nogant etc., etc.) were ever issued in a left hand version.

- Military Bull-pup rifles are now in use or under consideration by Britain and France. Steyr-Daimler-Puch in Austria produces a .223 Bull-pup called the "AUG" (for Army Universal Gun). None of these are issued in left hand versions though the latest British proposal includes an armorer's conversion kit for left handed shooters.

- The civilian market is another, and apparently insoluble problem. Short of making a left handed M-14 action (not impossible but the market would be limited) there is no solution save giving up 20% of the potential market.

5) As a privately financed R & D project, the sniper rifle has some problems. If we assume our normal 10 to 1 return hurdle and a $2 million program we need roughly a $20 million cumulative return to investors in 20 years or an average of $1 million per year. Using our standard market penetration maximum of 5% and maximum royalty to the partnership of 10% that implies an average market (military and civilian) of $200 million per year. The following

Memo regarding the Sirkis M33 sniper rifle. This was just proof of the innovative thinking that Detonics Manufacturing Corporation had.

In 1983 Nehemiah brought a Mossad operative to Detonics. Nehemiah and Sid gave the operative a tour of the facility. They then visited my school at Factoria Square. The operative was very impressed with my demonstration of Kung-Fu techniques. He commented that I was so natural with weapons and techniques that I must have trained from a very early age.

The 451 Detonics was an outstanding cartridge. It gave the 1911 a cartridge capable of power and energy never before imagined. It was originally conceived by a gunsmith named Jeffredo. I remembered reading an article on Jeffredo's 45 J-Mag. It was written by Dean Grennell in a mid-1970s Gun World magazine. The 45 J-Mag cases were made by trimming .30-06 or .308 brass and then the cases were reamed open to increase powder capacity and the necks had to be reamed open to accept .451 diameter bullets.

Sid mentioned to me that they had acquired the 45 J-Mag from Jeffredo and it became the 451 Detonics. Detonics did quite a bit of testing and discovered the best brass was made up from 45 Winchester Magnum brass. Sid showed me a picture of a very heavily loaded 451 Detonics made with modified 45 Winchester Magnum brass. Sid said that the unsafe powder charge did not blow up the case. The brass case looked very pregnant as the pressure blew outward the brass in the "unsupported" area.

So all the Detonics 451 Magnum cases were made by Winchester and custom stamped for Detonics Manufacturing Corporation.

The 451 Detonics conversion kits were outstanding. They exhibited high quality parts. Included with the kits were a match quality barrel, match quality barrel bushing, Detonics extractor, Detonics recoil system, reloading manual and reamer for use with 308 cases. The use of 30/06 brass was no longer recommended because of the different angle the rim had.

Unfortunately there was a run of "elliptical chamber" 451 Detonics conversion kits. A vendor had stamped the caliber over the chamber and did not use the proper procedure. The impact of the stamping caused the chamber to be minutely oval, or "elliptical." I purchased one of the kits and it fired fine. The unit functioned perfectly and there was no issue of the brass becoming out of spec.

The 451 Detonics Magnum was such a devastating round. I remember one of my students Mike Galanti, loading mid-powered rounds with my 45 caliber favorite bullet, the Speer 200 grain jacketed hollow point. I shot up a 2 liter Seven Up bottle, capped tight and full of water. It was about 15 yards away and I first shot it with four or five full metal jacket 9mm bullets from my Glock 17. Water just "glugged" out of the 2 liter bottle. I grabbed the 1911 Government Model with the 451 Detonics Magnum and fired one shot. The half filled 2 liter Seven Up bottle exploded! The bottle disappeared! Then falling back down to earth from high above was a sheet of green plastic. I came down floating down, swaying back and forth like a heavy feather.

I also received a letter from a university security guard that needed to shoot a rapid dog on campus with the 451 Detonics Magnum. He said it was so powerful that it immediately stopped the rapid dog. In fact he made reference how it turned the dog inside out.

Not a pretty picture as I was responding to his letter as the Technical Representative.

The Scoremaster was the company's attempt to get a product into the shooting sports. The pistol was created using the highest quality parts and used the cone barrel and recoil system with the Detonics' "elastomer" polymer to reduce the impact the frame would receive. If I remember correctly, the gunsmiths were trying to name it and Raul Bloom thought of the name Scoremaster. He owned one of the old Remington 22lr rifles and thought the name would fit with an IPSC pistol.

Original Scoremaster

Later on a Scoremaster with a "street" barrel and a barrel with a compensator mounted on it became a reality. The thought was the standard 5" barrel could be used for the "street" or for "limited class." The compensated barrel would be used for the "unlimited" class. Richard Niemer came up with the idea and named it the Janus Scoremaster. He thought of the Roman god of beginnings and transitions. This god is usually depicted as one with two faces, since he looks to the future and the past.

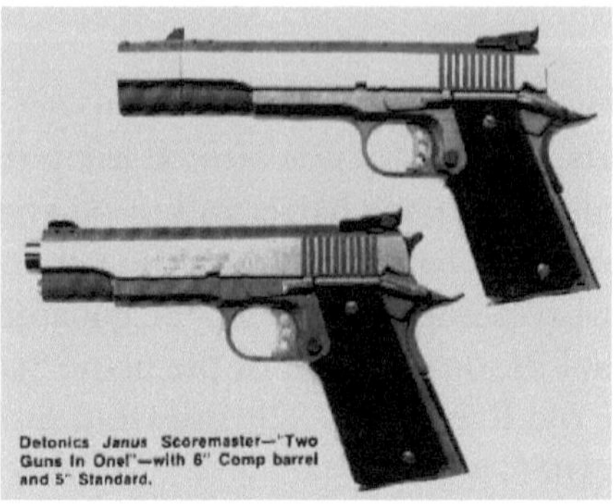

Detonics Janus Scoremaster

At the time when Detonics Manufacturing Corporation was putting together a shooting team, I was interested. I was approved to be a member and checked out a Scoremaster in 451 Detonics Magnum to be my IPSC match pistol. I knew the other members would shoot 45 acps, but I selected the over powered 451 Detonics Magnum to promote the pistol and our new cartridge. I had lots of experience with 44 magnums and did rapid fire with those handguns too.

I requested 200 rounds of 451 Detonics Magnum cartridges and went shooting one weekend with some of my students. We were up in hills of North Bend. Within 30 shots I blew the Millet front sight off. We searched for a bit and finally found the front sight. The speed and force of the slide acceleration sheared off the pin holding the front sight in place. I fired the remainder of the 200 rounds point shooting. I was still accurately placing bullets as I was looking over my pistol.

Author shooting an early Scoremaster in 451 Detonics Magnum in 1983. Notice the front sight is missing. "Peter Built" Combat Master rides in a belt slide holster.

I continued shooting all those magnum rounds to break in the new Scoremaster. It ran flawlessly. Later the gunsmiths went to two pins to hold in the front sight and also used Loctite.

TO: PAUL MARLOW
MIKE MAES
SID WOODCOCK
DIANE McCARTHY
JEFF GERBER

Alan good ideas — I do em! Paul

FROM: ALLEN J. CHINN

To promote the .451 Detonics Magnum in both the firearms and conversion units, I feel that these actions should be attempted:

1. Get ammo commercially manufactured. Factory loaded ammo, because of its unavailability, is our main stumbling block. I believe we should contact these companies:

a. Winchester
b. Remington
c. Federal
d. PMC
e. Speer
f. H & H Cartridge Corp.
g. Norma

2. If the above companies will not comply, we should get ammo manufactured elsewhere. (i.e. Browning had its shotgun, rifle, & pistol ammo done in Canada by Dominion; Auto Mag by a firm in Mexico; and Remington's Dove Load in Mexico.)

3. Contact Ruger to find out how they got Remington to produce ammo for their .357 Maximum.

4. Contact the following gun makers to manufacture barrels in .451 Detonics Magnum:

a. Thompson/Center
b. Merril
c. Sterling

5. Send conversion units and firearms to popular gun writers (i.e. John Wooters, Art Blatt, Dean Grenall, Howard French, etc.)

6. Get representation at the pin shoots and the straight wall cased silhouette matches.

7. Send units to be evaluated to American Rifleman's technical staff.

1983 memo regarding 451 Detonics Magnum promotion

8. Get unprimed brass prices lowered (i.e. packaging in paper boxes and shipping in MTM boxes only with kits and guns.)

9. Get Winchester or Remington to offer .451 Detonics brass as standard catalog items.

I hope that these suggestions will be helpful in the promotion of our firearms and conversion units.

Allen

I had the Canadian customs forms ready to fill out. I had second thoughts and decided that I should be home with my family and not up in Canada shooting an IPSC match. So early on, I removed myself from the team and turned in my Scoremaster match pistol.

Many times vendors would submit less than quality parts to our company. Sometimes they were out of specifications and other times they might have a defect. Many of the pistols that the production staff masterfully put together were with out of spec parts. They had to basically build a custom pistol each time out of spec parts were used.

One time frame castings were delivered to our company. However there was a defective shrinkage in the frame. It was consistent in all these defective frame castings. The engineers looked at it and the solution was to CNC machine a hole where the shrinkage was located. The next step would be to insert a matching stainless steel plug into the hole. The engineers stated that the plugged solution would not affect Combat Master frames for strength or durability.

About this time Richard Niemer built a beautiful Combat Master MK VI for my brother Steven. It had the high polished slide, his name engraved on the slide and gold plated rear sight base, hammer, trigger, slide stop and magazine release. It was cased in a factory wood presentation case. It was beautiful, but like Richard's regular quality work, it was accurate, reliable and had a great trigger pull. Beautiful and ornate, but still a fighting gun!

Steven Chinn with his custom Combat Master MK VI with gold plated accents in a factory wood presentation case

I was speaking to Paul Marlow one day and he told me how they came up with the Pocket Nine. He said, "We took an AMT Backup and reamed out the chamber to 9mm. We kept loading it one at a time, but it wouldn't blow up. And that's how we came up with the idea." I believe Nehemiah Sirkis was the main designer of this pistol. He created a modified Walther design and retained the blow back system.

The Pocket Nines kicked so hard that they originally broke the plastic grips. Micarta and aluminum were materials used later.

Combat Master and Pocket Nine comparison and features promotion

Detonics was coming out with another two new innovative designs. One would be a full size double action pistol in either 45 ACP or 451 Detonics Magnum. The other design was a heavy duty, top break revolver. The prototype was built in 45 Long Colt and massive. It had a top break design that utilized the "elastomer" polymer that the company had designed. It was truly impressive and featured high quality of materials and craftsmanship.

Detonics full size double action pistol

Detonics large caliber top break revolver

In 1983 Smith and Wesson came out to visit the Bellevue facility as they were possibly interested in acquiring Detonics. We believed they came out to scout for new ideas and learn about the processes that we used successfully to make an all stainless steel pistol that functioned. Smith and Wesson became famous for producing pistols after companies like Devel and Seventrees created custom S&W autos and did all the design, research and development.

I had numerous ideas that I thought the company should look at. I had suggested four 1911 variations.

My "Demon" model would be the company's Mark V model, but with a round butt frame and mainspring housing. Funny this "round butt" feature would show up 20 years later in various 1911 pistols. I also suggested a "finger extension" for the bottom of the six round magazines that would also act as a "bumper pad."

My "Warrior" model would be the company's Mark V or Mark VI, but it would include ambi-safety, long match trigger, extended slide stop and serrations on the trigger guard.

The "Nighthawk" model would use the company's Mark V or Mark VI slide assembly on a full size frame. The grip safety would be "melted" and deactivated. The reason for this model was a 1911 with a Combat Master short top end would provide the quickest draw. A full size frame would give the most control and more ammunition capacity.

1/10/83

TO: PAUL MARLON
MIKE MAES
SID WOODCOCK
DIANE McCARTHY
JEFF GERBER

FROM: ALLEN J. CHINN

The following are some suggestions that I hope can increase profits and help marketing:

1. Increase our product line to offer our customers greater variety in firearms, accessories, and services. This makes our company appear to be more vast and have greater depth.

*2. Market a Magazine Finger Extension/Bumper Pad. This would allow finger support to the small finger and would allow shooters greater reliability of the magazine being locked by the magazine lock catch upon quick reloading. This item should be make of a durable rubber material as it will also protect the magazine floor plate as magazines are dropped upon speed loading.

*3. The DETONICS DEMON is a round-butted MK V with corresponding stainless steel mainspring housing. The appearance and feel are impressive and should be in demand.

*4. WARRIOR Series are MK V or VI's with ambi-safety, extended long trigger, Pachmayr grips, extended magazine release, and serrated front trigger guard.

*5. NIGHTHAWK Series are Detonics top ends on full size frames. This modification would have a "melted" grip safety and tang. The grip safety would be operatable.

*6. The KINGPIN is a full size match auto in .451 Magnum and .45 ACP. It would be similiar to the Scoremaster except for:

a. 6" cone barrel with front sight mounted on it
b. hooked trigger guard, serrated in front
c. melted grip safety and tang
d. surface flutes on slide
e. Detonics ejection port
f. Mag-na-port optional

Memo regarding adding my design concepts, a convertible, 22lr conversion kit, knives, custom shop, law enforcement training and showroom

*7. Detonics Convertibles in 9MM/.38 Super, .45 ACP/9MM, or .45 ACP/.38 Super would be desireable and we'd sell many units. Interchangeable calibers have always been popular with shooters (i.e. Ruger Single-Six,Blackhawk models in 22 LR/22 MAG, 9MM/.357 MAG, and .45 ACP/.45 LC).

8. 22 LR Conversion Units would sell very well. With 18,000 units in the field, I'm sure we'd be able to sell this popular accessory. Up to now, L & B Metal Works, Van Nuys, CA., are the only people offering a custom conversion for Detonics, utilizing a Colt unit. Prices for the finished product were $400.00 or labor on the individual's unit would be $175.00. This was written about in Guns & Ammo, December 1980, as were the prices. I'm sure it's a marketable item if prices are reasonable.

*9. Detonics Knives would be great items to market. Shown in the drawing are small, very concealable knives that could be carried or kept anywhere. This is consistant with Detonics philosophy. The holster with a built-in sheath would be an innovation that would sell tremendously. This would allow an individual to carry his Detonics and a small knife at all times. These knives would be the only kind of its type.

10. A Detonics Custom Gun Shop (similar to Colt's) would increase shop revenue and allow customers to get the best work done on their Detonics. This also would bring in tremendous advertising and good public relations.

11. A Detonics Law Enforcement School (similar to Smith & Wesson's) on a special appointment basis would help in the areas of public relations with police and combat-oriented agencies. Firearms, weapons, and unarmed instruction would be given.

12. A showroom with accessories and weapons would be great for visiting customers, distributors, or officers. This could be set up at the reception office.

13. A small (Detonics size) double action .45 ACP would also be a tremendous seller. This would appeal to the left-handers and the double action lovers. I have seen a Seecamp converted Detonics MK I .45 ACP. It was very desireable to several of my past customers because of no need for manual safety use. With this product we could switch a lot of S & W users to our side.

14. Frankly, I think we should market the compact 9MM as soon as possible. This model would turn the market upside down. If we could get a pricing structure, we would be able to take pre-sold orders today! Like selling, the producing of the compact 9MM should be now, and with a firm commitment. Buyers don't always buy when there's too much time to think, but if we can get a commitment to establish a basis for doing business today...it could <u>and</u> should be done.

15. A Detonics Test Fire Day would be tremendous for promotion, advertising and public relations. This event would allow dealers, officers, distributors etc, to test fire specifically Detonic products for a ticket price. This would be similar to Warshall's and I have set up and co-ordinated such activities previously.

16. Get banks to consider Detonics for "Bank of Boulder" type investments.

17. A Detonics shooting tournament is also a good idea for public relations, promotion, and advertising. I also have experience in this area.

18. Finally, our catalog could be set up like Weatherby's $2.00 catalogs. Colorful, full of articles written by Weatherby and success stories by customers.

Thank you for taking the time to explore these ideas.

*See Attached Drawings

Allen

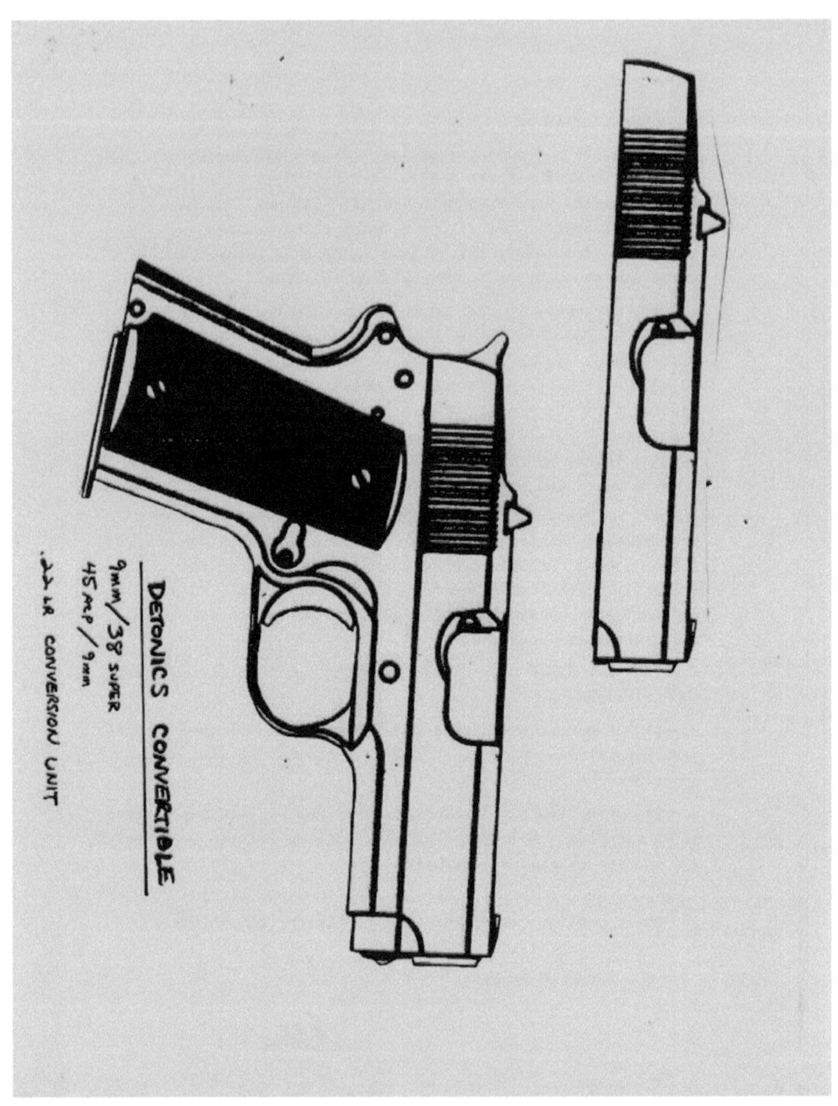

Detonics Combat Master Convertible suggestion

I also suggested a convertible Combat Master. We already offered a 45 ACP and 451 Detonics Magnum set. New interchangeable sets could include 9mm and 38 Super with barrel, magazine and recoil system. A 9mm and 45acp convertible would include a complete second top assembly, magazine and ejector in the second caliber. Finally I thought we should offer a set with a 22lr conversion kit included.

My "Kingpin" model would use a 5" slide and a 6" barrel, in 45 ACP or 451 Detonics Magnum. This pistol would be for bowling pin matches and could be used for hunting. The front sight would be mounted on the cone barrel. I drew up this concept before the Scoremaster was created. Other features would be a "hooked" trigger guard, surface flutes on the slide and optional Mag-na-porting.

I recommended personal defense weapons that would be hand held flashlights, but each of the three models would have a different special feature. One would shoot out tear gas, a second version would fire 22 cal pointed pellets or darts and be co2 powered. The third version would shoot out Speer 38 cal plastic bullets powered by pistol primers.

My recommendation for a 2 ½" barreled , four or five shot 410 gauge revolver was over 20 years before Taurus International built their Judge model. Even Smith and Wesson currently have their version called the Governor.

I also suggested a large version of the High Standard double action derringer. My version would have an enclosed trigger guard and made in 9mm and 45 ACP. The use of 1/3 moon clips would permit fast reloads as they would hold two shots ready to go.

New Product Ideas

1) Combat revolver – interchangable cylinder/barrel assemblies & grip frames. 5 shot 44 spl, 45LC 451 Det. Mag. – 6 shot 357 mag & 9mm. K frame size cylinder & grips contoured for use of S&W stocks. Barrel lengths 2½ & 4" (6" optional).

on white sheets ←

2) Double action – top break Derringer S.S. – similar to the Hi-Standard except longer frame to allow a full trigger guard. 45 ACP & 9mm are the calibers to be built first. These caliber would need the use of third moon clips or "double cartridge clips". We can produce interchangable calibers latter or offer them in other calibers upon acceptance of the market. Safer, more powerful & practical than anything available.

on White sheets ←

3) Single Shot S.S. Silhouette/Hunting Pistol
Similar to T/C except better lock-up configuration (Webly type), stainless steel and redesigned trigger guard. Slim profile like T/C. Will be successful because T/C's develope looseness after certain amount of use and are difficult to open. Ours won't be.
451 mag, 357 maximum, 44 mag, 30/30, etc... Uses T/C grips, scope mounts, etc.

4) Single Shot S.S. Rifle – basically the style would be a take off of gun #3 except with a thumb hole stock & 16" & ...

My hand written notes and ideas for possible products in 1983

10) <u>410 ga. Revolver</u> – a legally manufactured 410ga pistol. It would have rifling in the bore such as T/C's 45LC to make it a legal pistol and not a sawed off shotgun. This should be produced in a 4 or 5 shot 2½ 410ga. with ability to shoot 410ga. slugs. + Possibly with straight rifling

11) <u>PR-24 type flashlight</u> – a "C" cell flashlight with handle – to be marketed to law enforcement depts. with instruction on usage

12) <u>Riot Pike</u> – a 4 foot riot baton with a pike type head. It allows the officer to poke or hook the opponents leg to allow further control. This is to be marketed to law enf. with a book on techniques for applications.

13) <u>Detonics-port</u> – upside down triangle ports ▼ cut with EDM process to reduce recoil and muzzle jump.

14) <u>Detonics Leather</u> – ~~[illegible]~~ innovative leather ~~[illegible]~~ goods ~~[illegible]~~ with our logo on it. (I.E. ~~[illegible]~~ knife sheath-holster combo, leather designed for women etc....)

15) <u>Detonics Knives</u> – innovative knives with our name on it (combat & defense oriented)

16) <u>Finger extension / Bumper pad</u> – rubber bumper

5) Pocket Flare gun without light — same as on #4 white sheets except no flashlight. Omitting the light will allow one to two shots more. To be constructed of plastic for light weight & durability.

6) Pocket Defense Light — same as on #5 white sheets except fires .22 cal darts or .22 cal pointed pellets (i.e. Beeman Silver Jet) Powered by CO_2 cartridges, but will need special "O" rings for prolonged storage in ready position.

7) Pocket Defense Light — Same as #5 white sheets except shoots nails ~~[illegible]~~ powered by ~~[illegible]~~ ~~[illegible]~~ 22 cal nail driving blanks. This weapon should be designed and produced with intension to sell to special law enforcement depts. and the government.

8) Pocket Defense Light — Same as above except shoots flechettes powered by CO_2. Again to be marketed to special enforcement depts and the government.

9) Same as all ~~[illegible]~~ the pocket weapons except to be produced as a disposable, factory pre-loaded weapon. Not reloadable and super simple for anyone to use. All self contained.

I also thought a collection of concealable fixed bladed fighting knives would be profitable to the company.

Richard Niemer and I proposed a custom gun shop to not only customize Detonics products, but to also work on all the general 1911 needs of customers.

TO: MIKE MAES
SID WOODCOCK
PAUL MARLOW
DIANE McCARTHY
JEFF GERBER

FROM: ALLEN CHINN

DATE: FEBRUARY 14, 1983

SUBJECT: DETONICS CUSTOM GUN SHOP

THIS MEMO IS TO ELABORATE ON THE SUGGESTION OF THE DETONICS CUSTOM GUN SHOP PER MY MEMO ON 1/10/83.

THE DETONICS CUSTOM GUN SHOP WOULD INCREASE REVENUE, CASH FLOW, PUBLIC RELATIONS, AND PROSPECTIVE CUSTOMER AWARENESS. THE INITIAL INVESTMENT TO START THE D.C.G.S. WOULD BE VERY MINOR, AS WE ALREADY HAVE MOST OF THE EQUIPMENT NEEDED. THE PROFITS AND INCOME FROM THE D.C.G.S. COULD BE CONSIDERABLE AS MONEY WOULD BE RECEIVED FOR ALL LABOR, PARTS, AND ACCESSORIES.

HERE IS A BASIC OUTLINE OF POSSIBLE WORK AND SERVICES IN RESPECT TO IMPORTANCE AND ABILITY TO GET THIS PROGRAM INTO ACTION:

THE DETONICS CUSTOM GUN SHOP

PHASE I (AVAILABLE AT THIS TIME)

A. SERVICES

1. AUTO PISTOLS (1911 AND VARIANTS)

A. TRIGGER JOBS
B. SIGHT INSTALLATIONS
C. BARREL AND BUSHING INSTALLATIONS
D. BEVEL MAGAZINE WELLS
E. THROAT & POLISH FEED RAMP
F. LOWER EJECTION PORTS
G. .451 DETONICS MAGNUM CONVERSIONS

Follow up memo regarding a proposed Detonics Custom Gun Shop

H. Ambidextrious safety installations
I. Overhauls, combat tune jobs, etc...

B. Part Sales

1. Auto Pistols

A. Barrels
B. Bushings
C. Extractors
D. Recoil systems
E. .451 Detonics Magnum Conversion Units
F. Sights (Bomar, Millet, Detonics, etc..)
G. Extended grip safeties
H. Extended magazine releases
I. Ambidextrious safeties
J. Rounded magazine followers
K. Adjustable long triggers
L. Ejectors
M. Hammers
N. Stainless magazines
O. Internal lock work parts, etc...

Note, we can set up individual custom work requests as well as custom work packages. Packages would include a variety of parts and accessories installed with custom modifications.

Phase II (Future possibilities)

A. Services

1. Auto pistols

A. As mentioned in Phase I
B. Working on other makes (i.e., Browning, S & W)

2. Revolvers

A. Combat tunes
B. Barrel and frame cut-downs

PG 3

C. CONVERSIONS, ETC...

3. REFINISHING

A. BLUEING
B. HARD CHROME
C. ELECTROLESS NICKEL

4. PORTING

A. MAG-NA-PORT
B. DETONIC-PORT (OUR VARIATION OF MAG-NA-PORT)

B. PART SALES

1. AUTO PISTOLS

A. AS MENTIONED IN PHASE I
B. SIMILAR TO ABOVE, EXCEPT FOR BROWNING, S & W ETC...

2. REVOLVERS

A. SIGHTS (BOMAR, MILLET, ETC...)
B. LOCK WORK PARTS
C. CONVERSION KITS
D. SPRING KITS
E. BARRELS, ETC...

THE D.C.G.S. WOULD HAVE TREMEMDOUS MARKET POTENTIAL AS CAN BE SEEN IN THE MANY DISPLAY ADVERTISEMENTS CURRENTLY SHOWN IN THE POPULAR GUN MAGAZINES. OUR ADVANTAGE WOULD BE THAT WE ARE RECOGNIZED AS A COMBAT ORIENTED COMPANY, WE DO HAVE CUSTOM PISTOLS ON A PRODUCTION BASIS AND WE ARE RECOGNIZED AS A MAJOR MANUFACTURER OF COMBAT FIREARMS. THE PEOPLE INTERESTED IN CUSTOM WORK IN THE FIELD OF COMBAT AND POLICE PISTOLS WILL DEFINITELY TAKE THE DETONICS CUSTOM GUN SHOP INTO CONSIDERATION.

Pg 4

I truly believe that we can take lots of orders and make lots of money with the custom shop. Phase I can be put into action today! With only minor advertising (i.e. flyers, mailers, etc...), we can make it very successful in a relatively short time.

Phase II would make a well-rounded custom shop that would give the combat shooter almost every service needed. This would increase income over Phase I, but would need investments for equipment.

Thank you for taking the time to explore the Detonics Custom Gun Shop. Please let me know what you think of it and your feelings toward this matter.

Thanks! Allen

Allen

***Please review attachments.

After the development of the new Detonics Top Break Revolver, I suggested to create a smaller "K" frame size with interchangeable barrels and grip frames. This size would be handier for daily carry and there were so many holsters already in the market. I proposed a 5 shot top break in 451 Detonics Magnum that could also shoot the shorter 45 ACP cartridge. I also thought a 6 shot top break in 9mm would be successful. Both pistols would use full moon clips.

With the top break mechanism already developed, I thought a silhouette and hunting pistol, as well as a carbine/rifle could be successful. These firearms could also be used as tactical precision weapons capable taking out targets at medium to long range. These would also be very easy to suppress. I was named co-inventor of the silhouette and hunting pistol.

I also submitted a suggestion to build a left hand bolt action "Remington XP100 style" silhouette pistol. The thought was to build a repeater for right handed shooters. The shooting hand would not move and the left hand would work the bolt, reloading rapidly as needed. These pistols would also be very easy to suppress.

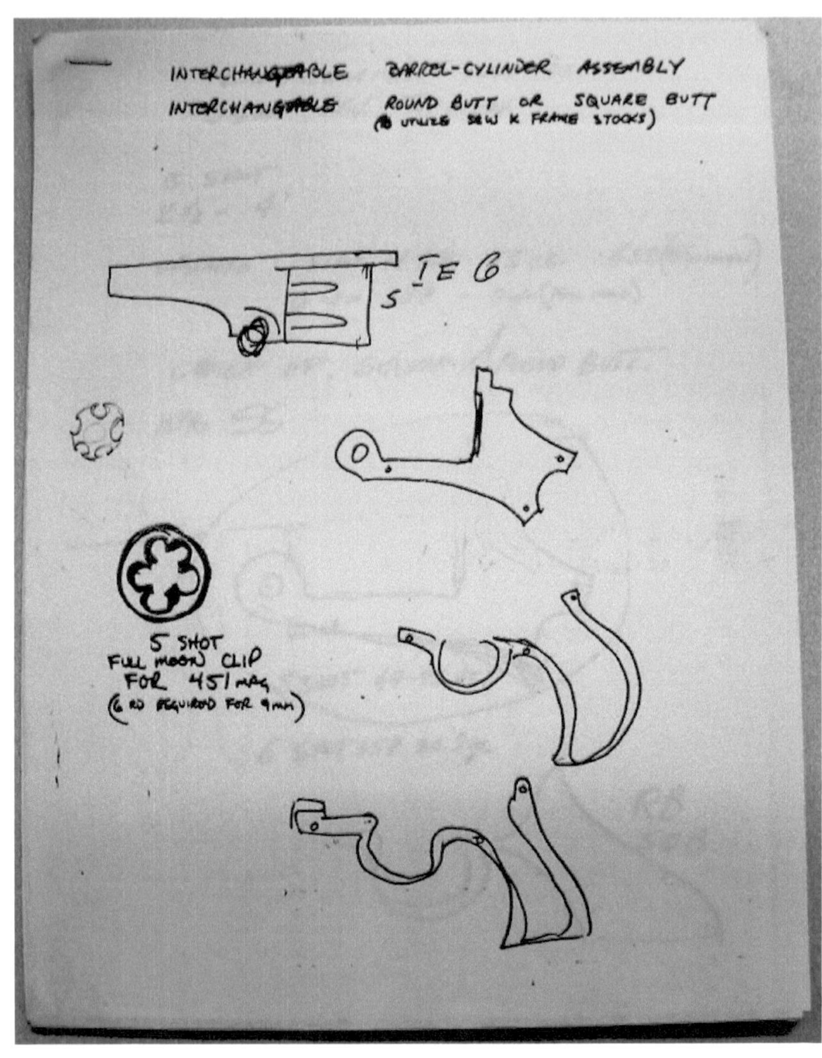

Top break revolver ideas for a "K" frame sized revolver with interchangeable grip frames and barrels. Use with full moon clips for a five shot 451 Detonics Magnum and a six shot 9mm.

MEMO

TO: MIKE MAES
SID WOODCOCK
PAUL MARLOW
DIANE McCARTHY
JEFF GERBER

FROM: ALLEN CHINN

DATE: FEBRUARY 1, 1983

RE: DEVELOPMENT SUGGESTIONS

1. WE SHOULD HAVE OUR TRADEMARK STAMPED ON ALL OUR WEAPONS. MANY CUSTOMERS DON'T REALIZE THAT WE EVEN HAVE A LOGO. COLT HAS THEIR STALLION; SMITH & WESSON WITH THEIR S & W INSIGNIA; RUGER HAS THEIR EAGLE, ETC.....WE SHOULD MAKE OUR TRADEMARK RECOGNIZED.

2. I'VE BEEN THINKING ABOUT HOW WE CAN GET INTO THE LAW ENFORCEMENT MARKET. POLICE FIREARMS HAVE ALWAYS BEEN A DEPARTMENT "RECOMMENDATION" AS FAR AS CIVILLIANS ARE CONCERNED. ONE PROPOSAL IS A POLICE FIREARMS TRADE-IN PROGRAM. WHAT THIS PROGRAM ALLOWS THE DEPARTMENT TO DO IS TRADE IN THEIR OLD FIREARMS IN ON NEW DETONICS (CURRENTLY NOT TO INCLUDE THE THREE NEW WEAPONS). THE PREDETERMINED TRADE IN ALLOWANCE WOULD BE CREDITED AGAINST THE POLICE PRICE OF THE NEW FIREARMS. THE LOTS OF TRADE IN GUNS WOULD THEN BE TURNED LOOSE TO THE NATIONAL RIFLE ASSOCIATION (OR ANY OTHER OUTFIT) FOR A SLIGHT PROFIT. THE NRA, FOR EXAMPLE, COULD OFFER THESE POLICE GUNS TO THEIR MEMBERS AT VERY REASONABLE PRICES. THE MAIN PURPOSE OF THIS PROGRAM IS TO:

A. GET INTO THE LAW ENFORCEMENT MARKET
B. ACCEPT TRADE-INS WHILE STILL MAKING GOOD PROFITS
C. TAKE COMPETITIVE FIREARMS OUT OF THE DEPARTMENTS AND REPLACE THEM WITH OURS; AND,
D. DISPOSE OF COMPETITIVE FIREARMS AT A SLIGHT PROFIT

Memo regarding branding, police markets and instructional books

PG 2

WHAT PROMPTED ME TO COME UP WITH THIS IDEA WAS KIRKLAND P.D.'S INQUIRY ABOUT 25 TO 30 9MM'S IN OUR WEAPONS. THIS ALONG WITH NUMEROUS INDIVIDUAL INQUIRIES FROM OFFICERS WANTING OUR FIREARMS AS OFF-DUTY OR UNDERCOVER WEAPONS GAVE ME INCENTIVE TO COME UP WITH THIS POSSIBLE PROGRAM.

A POSSIBLE DISPOSITION LIST IS:

A. NRA
B. SECURITY AGENCIES
C. SMALLER POLICE DEPARTMENTS
D. GUN CLUBS
E. RETAIL STORES; AND,
F. POLICE DISTRIBUTORS

I BELIEVE THIS PROGRAM CAN BE PROFITABLE TO US BOTH IN DOLLARS AND IN PUBLIC RELATIONS.

3. BOOKS AND MANUALS CONCERNING SUBJECTS THAT ARE RELATED TO SELF-DEFENSE AND COMBAT ARE HIGH POTENTIAL MONEY MAKERS. OHARA PUBLICATIONS HAVE OVER 65 BOOKS ON SELF-DEFENSE AND MARTIAL ARTS. UNIQUE PUBLICATIONS ALSO HAS DOZENS OF MARTIAL ARTS BOOKS ON THE MARKET. A PUBLISHER WITH A DIVERSE VARIETY ON ARMED AND UNARMED COMBAT SUBJECT MATTER IS PALLADIN PRESS. THEIR BOOKS COVER EVERYTHING FROM KNIVES AND KICKS TO SILENCERS AND EXPLOSIVES (WE DON'T NEED TO BE THIS RADICAL).

I PROPOSE A SERIES OF BOOKS TO INSTRUCT THE FOLLOWING TARGET GROUPS:

A. CIVILLIANS

1. MALE
2. FEMALE
3. CHILDREN
4. ELDERLY
5. BUSINESS PEOPLE

PG 3

B. LAW ENFORCEMENT

1. PATROL
2. UNDERCOVER

THESE BOOKS CAN COVER ALL PHASES OF ARMED AND UNARMED SELF-DEFENSE AND COMBAT: FROM ELEMENTARY BASICS TO ADVANCED THEORY AND TACTICS. THESE BOOKS SHOULD DO VERY WELL IN SALES AND BROADEN OUR MARKET.

IT HAS ALSO BEEN MENTIONED TO ME THAT THERE IS AN IDEA ALONG THE SAME LINES EXCEPT IN VIDEO TAPES. I THINK THIS IS A WONDERFUL IDEA WHICH SHOULD BE VERY SUCCESSFUL.

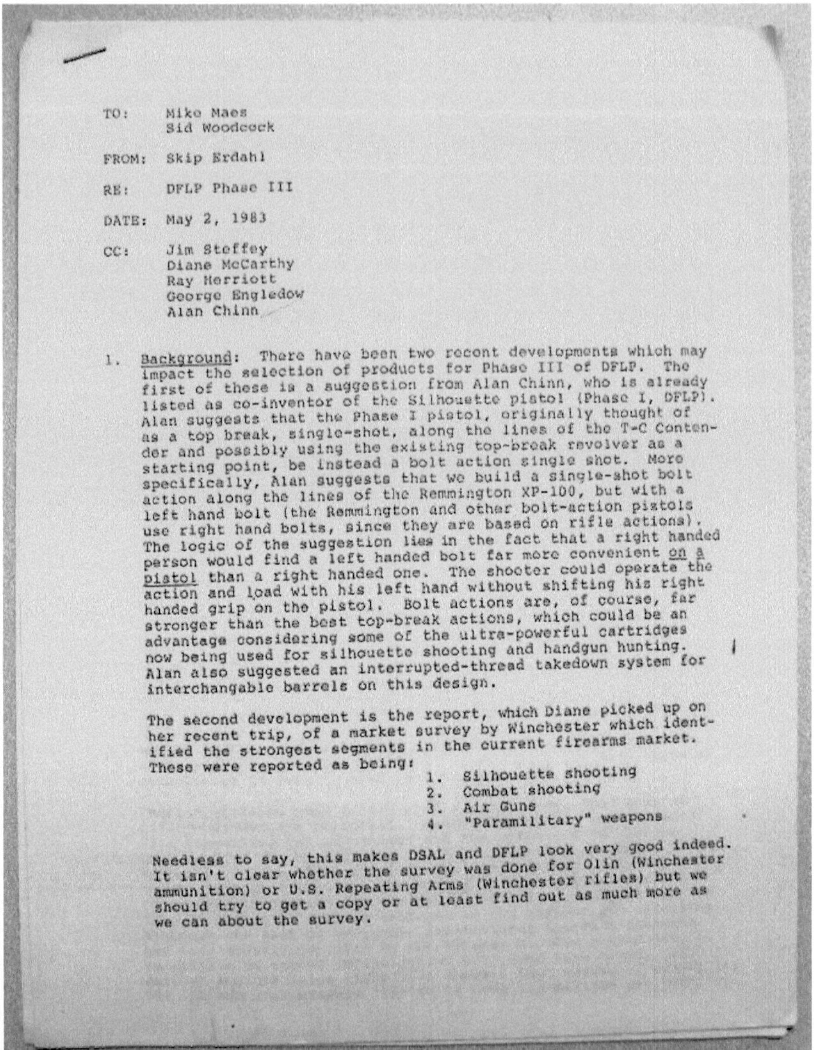

TO: Mike Maes
Sid Woodcock

FROM: Skip Erdahl

RE: DFLP Phase III

DATE: May 2, 1983

CC: Jim Steffey
Diane McCarthy
Ray Herriott
George Engledow
Alan Chinn

1. Background: There have been two recent developments which may impact the selection of products for Phase III of DFLP. The first of these is a suggestion from Alan Chinn, who is already listed as co-inventor of the Silhouette pistol (Phase I, DFLP). Alan suggests that the Phase I pistol, originally thought of as a top break, single-shot, along the lines of the T-C Contender and possibly using the existing top-break revolver as a starting point, be instead a bolt action single shot. More specifically, Alan suggests that we build a single-shot bolt action along the lines of the Remmington XP-100, but with a left hand bolt (the Remmington and other bolt-action pistols use right hand bolts, since they are based on rifle actions). The logic of the suggestion lies in the fact that a right handed person would find a left handed bolt far more convenient on a pistol than a right handed one. The shooter could operate the action and load with his left hand without shifting his right handed grip on the pistol. Bolt actions are, of course, far stronger than the best top-break actions, which could be an advantage considering some of the ultra-powerful cartridges now being used for silhouette shooting and handgun hunting. Alan also suggested an interrupted-thread takedown system for interchangable barrels on this design.

The second development is the report, which Diane picked up on her recent trip, of a market survey by Winchester which identified the strongest segments in the current firearms market. These were reported as being:

1. Silhouette shooting
2. Combat shooting
3. Air Guns
4. "Paramilitary" weapons

Needless to say, this makes DSAL and DFLP look very good indeed. It isn't clear whether the survey was done for Olin (Winchester ammunition) or U.S. Repeating Arms (Winchester rifles) but we should try to get a copy or at least find out as much more as we can about the survey.

Memo confirming me as co-inventor of a Detonics Silhouette pistol and my suggestions for a bolt action version

The sales manager blamed me for his failed consignment program. I was the scapegoat for his inability to produce sales. I remember overhearing that the consignment program was a fiasco that I created.

Shortly thereafter the sales manager took me into one of the offices and said, "I don't know how to say this, but it was either me or you. Sorry you have to go." He shook my hand good bye and I was laid off.

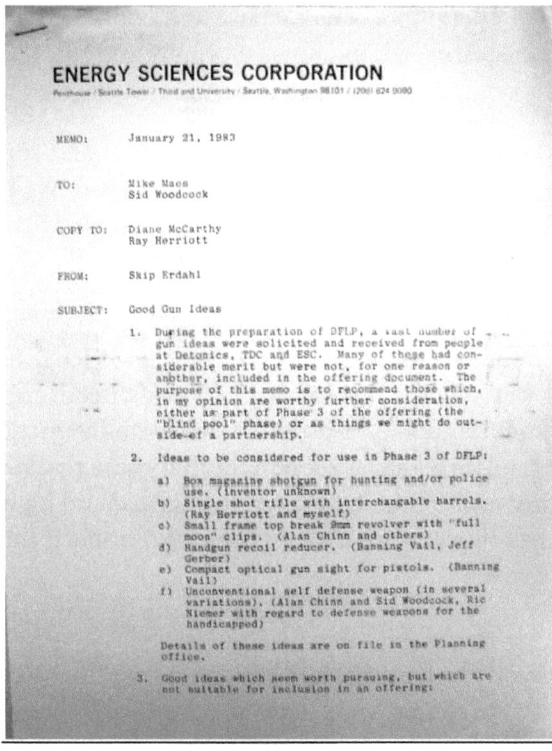

ENERGY SCIENCES CORPORATION

Penthouse / Seattle Tower / Third and University / Seattle, Washington 98101 / (206) 624 9090

MEMO: January 21, 1983

TO: Mike Maes
Sid Woodcock

COPY TO: Diane McCarthy
Ray Herriott

FROM: Skip Erdahl

SUBJECT: Good Gun Ideas

1. During the preparation of DFLP, a vast number of gun ideas were solicited and received from people at Detonics, TDC and ESC. Many of these had considerable merit but were not, for one reason or another, included in the offering document. The purpose of this memo is to recommend those which, in my opinion are worthy further consideration, either as part of Phase 3 of the offering (the "blind pool" phase) or as things we might do outside of a partnership.

2. Ideas to be considered for use in Phase 3 of DFLP:

a) Box magazine shotgun for hunting and/or police use. (inventor unknown)
b) Single shot rifle with interchangable barrels. (Ray Herriott and myself)
c) Small frame top break 9mm revolver with "full moon" clips. (Alan Chinn and others)
d) Handgun recoil reducer. (Banning Vail, Jeff Gerber)
e) Compact optical gun sight for pistols. (Banning Vail)
f) Unconventional self defense weapon (in several variations). (Alan Chinn and Sid Woodcock, Ric Niemer with regard to defense weapons for the handicapped)

Details of these ideas are on file in the Planning office.

3. Good ideas which seem worth pursuing, but which are not suitable for inclusion in an offering:

A few of my ideas were included in this memo regarding "Good Gun Ideas"

CHAPTER 7

Life after Detonics

After my departure from Detonics I was still working on my guns and gun ideas. I continued teaching Kung-Fu. My knowledge and abilities increased as I became close friends with the Sifus up in Canada. I trained harder and developed greater skills

I received my Federal Firearms License and continued acquiring and creating customized handguns, shotguns and rifles.

I maintained my friendship with Richard Niemer and sometimes I would come and visit the Detonics facility. Most times I would miss Sid as he was busy as usual and I had a full time job as a Recreation Professional with the City of Seattle.

Richard continued to work on 1911 and his knowledge and skills increased. I was still buying Combat Masters whenever my funds would permit me to do so. I found a Mark I and later a Mark V that he masterfully rebuilt. I remember that these two pistols did not group very well. I brought them to Richard and he noticed the slide and barrel fit were not the best. He also noticed that the slides were a "little soft."

Richard replaced the barrels and slides with ones that were a better fit. He also tuned the recoil system. Both pistols were now prime examples of the Combat Master. When I took them to the Seattle

Police Athletic Association Range, they both made fist size groups at 25 yards. I was very happy with these offhand groups.

He built an outstanding Combat Master Mark I that had floral engraving and had the Soldier of Fortune logo engraved on the top of the slide. The "Soldier of Fortune" is very rare, as Detonics only had a few of the slides made for a Soldier of Fortune shoot. He also built a customized Servicemaster on a 70s series forged Colt frame. He also worked on a Colt series 70, 38 Super for me. His work was always top quality and he always paid attention to the smallest detail.

Rare engraved "Soldier of Fortune" Combat Master MK I

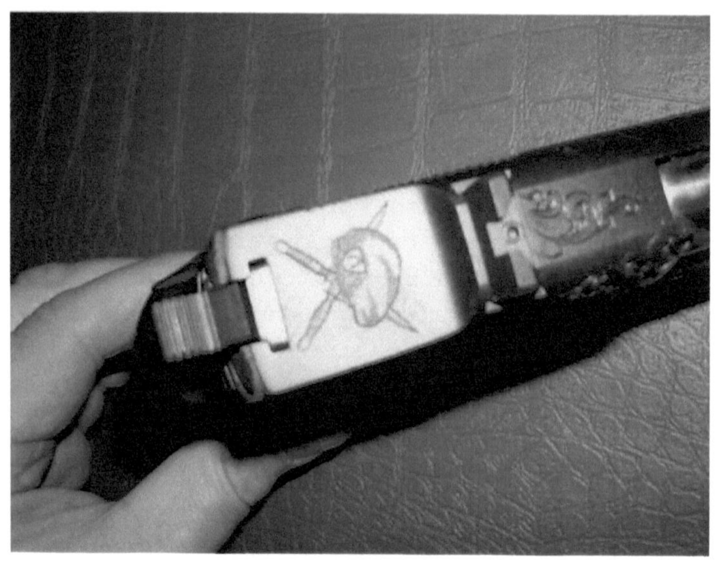

Rare engraved "Soldier of Fortune" Combat Master MK I

Custom Niemer Detonics Servicemaster slide on series 70 Colt frame

I had written to several firearm magazines and a couple responded that they would be interested in me writing articles for them. I came back to Detonics one afternoon and took pictures of Richard and his 1911 handiwork. I also took pictures of Chuck McGough and the shooting tube.

Richard Niemer holding one of his custom compensated 1911s in 1987

Chuck McGough working on a Combat Master in 1987

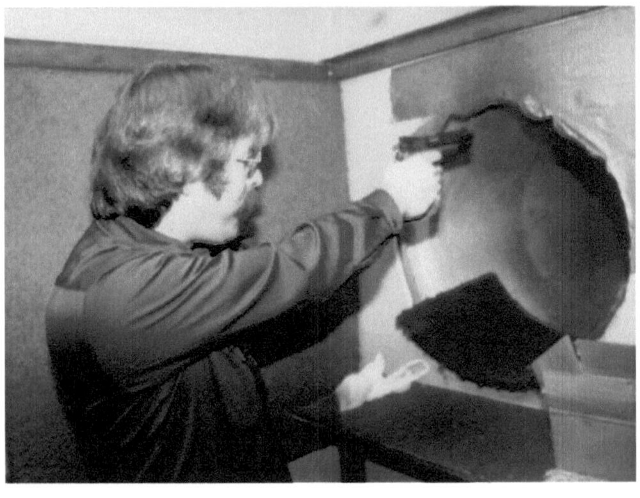

Richard Niemer test firing at the "shooting tube" at the Bellevue facility

Over the years I have come into contact with Detonics aficionados. Many are interested in getting a good deal on a great Combat Master. Some are interested in unique pieces that have collective value.

I met Doug Barnes through my auctions on the Internet. He is a very serious collector and among the firearms that he collects, Detonics is amongst them. He purchased my "Soldier of Fortune" engraved Combat Master, my Servicemaster Detonics/Colt custom, my Colt series 70 38 Super/Detonics Prototype and my Detonics papers and files from the early 1980s.

Amongst his collection was Sid's personal Combat Master with the custom serial number "SID."

Sid's personal Combat Master serial number "SID"

Here was the auction description that accompanied this pistol:

Serial # SID is one of a kind. Because it was made for Sid Woodcock by the production staff, they wanted it to be as good as it could be. The actual gunsmith spent months putting this firearm together. All the parts were blueprinted and specked for a tight fit and lapped into place. The trigger guard was heated and slightly stretched to flatten the front strap. At the time, they did not have the tools to use power sanders and buffers to create a "parade grade" finish. The gunsmith ended up sanding and polishing all the parts by hand. Most of them on a surface plate so all the lines would be sharp and straight. An 800 grit Emory cloth was used for the final finish. Philosophy, the Problem, and the Solution In all of human history, one of the most honorable and valuable activities has always been to help others save their own lives. This activity has come in many forms, with ancient Japanese sword makers having the social status of a deity, second only to the god-emperor. In the modern age, the closest analog to the samurai's sword maker is the combat handgun designer. Unlike the sword makers, most all handgun designers in history have never been in combat, have never used their design for its intended purpose, and fundamentally don't understand the subtleties of requirement for this function. Also, only one known firearm designer in human history has also been granted the title of Grand Master in Chun Na. Thus, most 'combat' and 'professional' handguns fall far short of the need, even today. A young man volunteered for service in early WWII, after having grown up in Arizona and Idaho. As a child, he met and spoke with Sheriff Wyatt Earp, and was trained in several styles of Asian martial arts by Chinese immigrants. Though underage, he was accepted into the Army, and rapidly saw service in combat. His skill and ability was noticed by 'talent spotters' and was soon recruited to work with the OSS, becoming friends with Willie Fairbairn, Rex Applegate and others. He served both in Europe and in China during that war, and personally helped to save the world, multiple times. Unlike most all others in Detachment 101, he survived. He continued to serve in every conflict the USA engaged in from 1945 through the 1980s. An amazing story, to this date almost completely untold although touching all of us, had formed. After over 30 years of active service to this country, including the US Army, OSS, and under contract to AEC, CIA, DOD, FBI, DOJ, and mostly as a 'consultant' provided by the US Government to selected individuals and groups around the world for 'special projects and needs', Mr. Sid Woodcock decided to focus his completely unique understanding, experience and abilities on a new project. After having used all of the modified M1911 handguns in existence and found them wanting, and having been offered one of them through his work with Explosives Corporation of America in Redmond, WA, Mr. Woodcock found himself sitting on a beach in Central America in 1973, with an idea. Though on a sanctioned job, he found himself with the operational need for a handgun that didn't exist, and with a business opportunity to create it. The requirement was clear: design, manufacture and supply the most compact, concealable, reliable, accurate, powerful and adaptable handgun in the world. The concept of the Detonics Combat Master had thus been born. Combat Master features Under Mr. Woodcock's direction, and due to his unique background, the Combat Master introduced multiple features, some of them patented. These features have become standard on the world's best handguns, and were introduced to the world on this very gun. Several were invented by Mr. Woodcock. Three-dot sights, the coned barrel, no barrel bushing, beveled magazine well, cocking relief, tuned trigger pull, tuned recoil impulse, loaded magazine indicator, ejection port relief, enhanced extractor geometry, fouling-resistant internal design, captive recoil system, 100% no-tools disassembly and reassembly, no loaded springs upon disassembly 'field safe' design, no grip-safety, drop-test safe, polished ramp and flared chamber, lowered bore axis, and more; all were incorporated together into a production gun for the first time in history, in this specific Combat Master. Later, the Detonics Combat Master offered the world's first 100% stainless steel handgun with no metallurgic or functioning problems. All stainless steel handguns in the world, today, directly stem from this legacy. Even today, over 35 years after original design, the Combat Master remains the iconic and pre-eminent 'designed for personal combat by a veteran operator' handgun. Many of the world's most highly trained and sophisticated professionals continue to use and rely on the Combat Master for their most important mission: self-defense. Even today, the Combat Master has no peer.

I double checked with Sid, not sure if this piece was a counterfeit or fraud. Sid confirmed to me it was in fact his and a friend was helping him sell it. Doug was able to win this very valuable piece.

Doug also was able to procure other very special pieces. Amongst his collection, he has a Detonics Speedmaster that was won by past IPSC President Dave Stanford. He was the 1988 Washington State Champion.

Detonics Speedmaster engraved 1988 Washington State Champion Dave Stanford

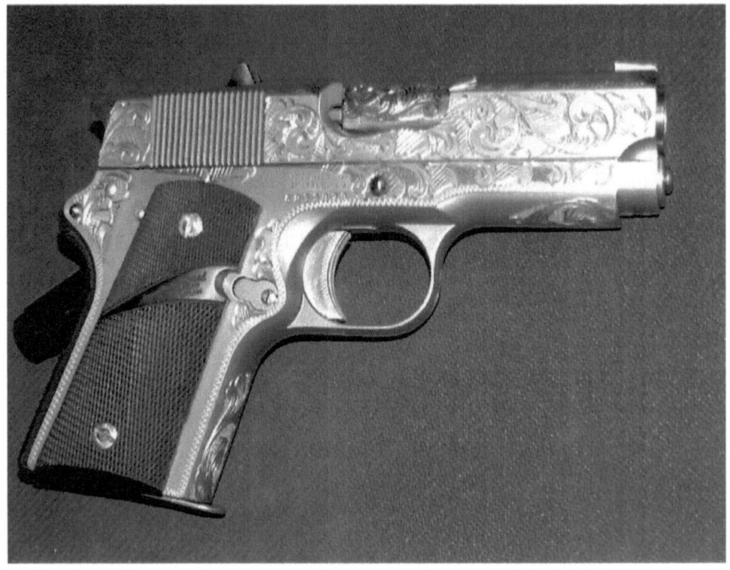

Custom engraved Combat Master by Jeff Flannery

Custom Detonics Street Master with 5" and 6" barrels

Doug procured a beautiful Combat Master custom engraved by Jeff Flannery. Also included in his Detonics collection is a special four barrel Street Master set. The fitted barrels include five and six inch barrels in 45 ACP and five and six inch barrels in 451 Detonics Magnum.

Seattle based Detonics gunsmith Scotty Meeker was accredited with the creation of the Street Master. He liked the longer sight radius and increased velocity of the longer slide. However, he liked the shorter grip frame of the Combat Master for concealment.

CHAPTER 8

Sid's Simple Pleasures

Whenever I entered his apartment I could see his numerous pictures that adorned the walls near his kitchen and hallway. He had a passion for photography. I remembered that he purchased a new camera just a couple of years ago. He was pleased with the new technology and the small handy size.

The photographs on his wall were amazing. Many were pictures that he took while off to far off lands. Some were of local landmarks. Several photographs of ancient structures were present. A couple of them were of the beautiful form of young women.

The ones in his hallway were remarkable photographs. Some were of prototype munitions, an atomic energy plant and evidence of bombings.

Some held special memories that only Sid knew. We can only guess why he had a photograph of a boxed Browning Renaissance Set, that included a Browning Hi Power 9mm pistol, a Browning 1955 380 pistol and a "Baby" Browning 25acp pistol all in Renaissance style engraving featuring a vine and floral pattern.

What stories were hidden in the picture with Che Guevara, Errol Flynn and Castro? Sid spent time as a CIA contractor in Central and South America. Only Sid knew the truth.

Sid's wall picture #1

Sid's wall picture #2

Sid's wall picture #3

Sid's wall picture #4

Sid's wall picture #5

Sid's wall picture #6

Sid's wall picture #7

Sid's wall picture #8

Sid's wall picture #9

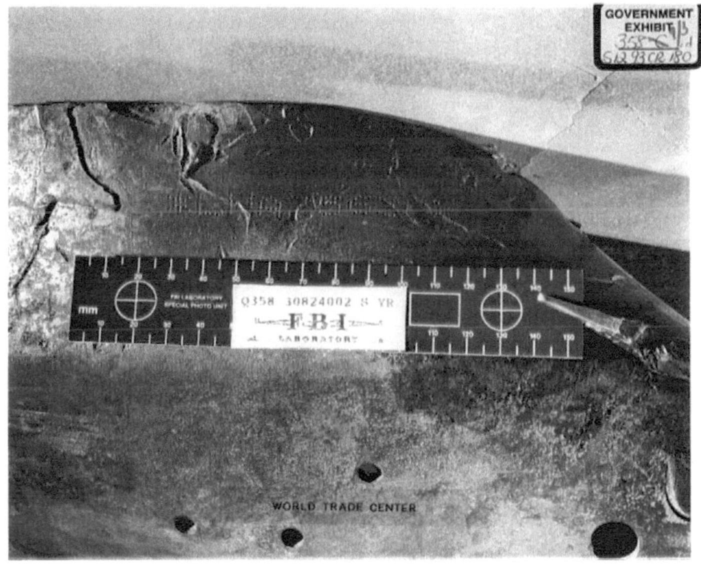

Sid's wall picture #10

Sid's wall picture #11

Sid's wall picture #12

Sid's wall picture #13

Among Sid's simple pleasures were a glass of wine, dark chocolate and visits with his family and friends.

CHAPTER 9

Sid's Passing

On June 24th last year my 76 year old student Jack Mattison sent me a message on Facebook that he had heard Sifu Woodcock has just passed away. He knew that I was very close to him.

I was in shock as Kregg Jorgenson, my son Brandon and I just visited him a few weeks earlier on his 87th birthday. I brought him dim sum and my latest book at the time "Ladies Fight Back."

I searched on the Internet and saw several posts that stated he recently had passed away. I didn't know what to do. So I left a message on Sid's answering machine.

I was deeply saddened to have learned of his passing. His family and students did not know how to get in touch with me.

A week later I received a call from Dale Larsen. He told me they checked Sid's answering machine and were sorry they didn't know how to get in touch with me. He also mentioned that I had missed the memorial service.

I later received a call from Sid's daughter-in-law Thelma. She and I spoke for quite some time.

I will miss his conclusion to our phone calls. I would usually call to see how he was doing and to make arrangements to visit him. He would usually end the conversations by saying "Look forward to seeing you old friend."

Knowing Sid was a rare privilege. I am highly honored to have known him and become his close friend.

I and everyone else have been richer for having him in our lives. Our wonderful memories of him will always live within us.

Sid's daughter Connie Ortiz

<u>Sid's Family and Friends (from left to right)</u>

Robert Jaeger - friend and professional associate

Connie Ortiz - daughter

Phyllis Larson – friend

Thelma Mosebar – daughter-in-law

Bob Mosebar - son

Pani Saleh - friend

Todd Mosebar - grandson

Sue Madlinger - friend

In
Memory Of
Sidney Herbert Woodcock
May 29, 1924 – June 5, 2011
Father, Grandfather
Friend and Sensei
His last message reads:
"To all my family and friends, I want
to thank you all for your support
through the years. You have made
life great. Could not have done it
without you. I am now going to look
into another world. In short, another
adventure. Love you all and wish you
all the very best, Sid."

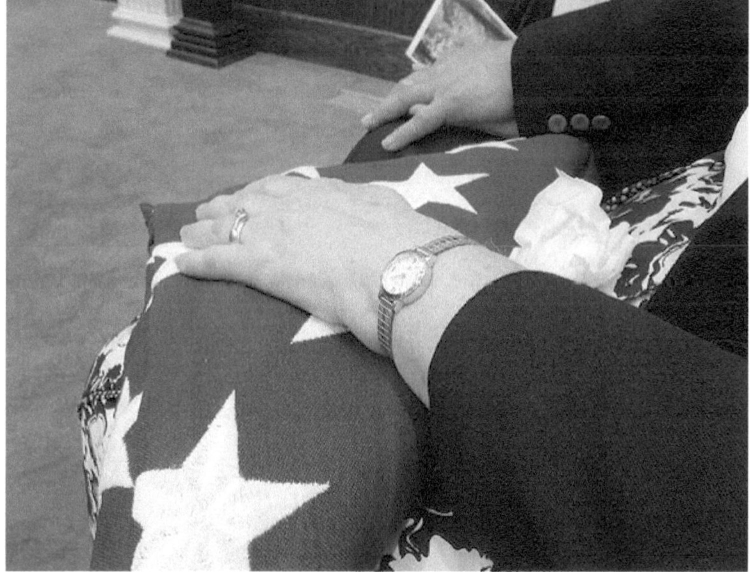

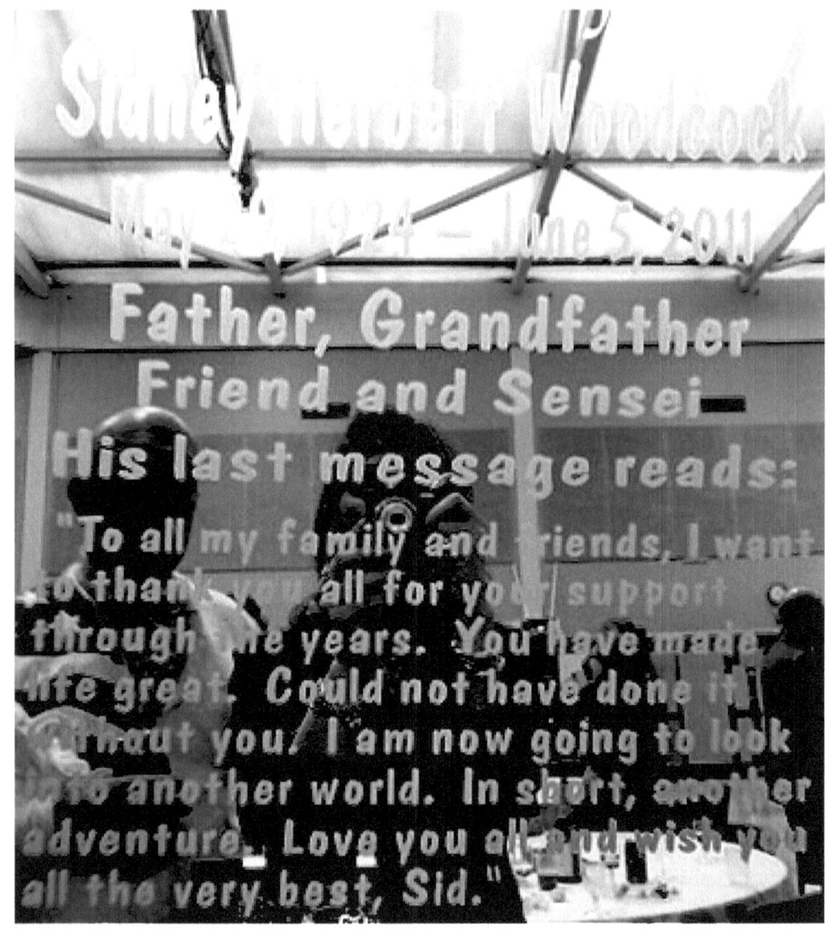

Woodcock
1924 – June 5, 2011
Father, Grandfather
Friend and Sensei
His last message reads:
"To all my family and friends, I want
all for your support
years. You have made
Could not have done it
you. I am now going to look
another world. In short, another
adventure. Love you all and wish you
all the very best, Sid."

Sid's son Bob Mosebar and daughter-in-law Thelma

In early January of 2012, I was able to meet with Bob and Thelma Mosebar at their lovely home. They were wonderful and we spent seven hours talking about Sid and his stories. It was Bob's willingness to include his father's pictures that enriched this book.

CHAPTER 10

Epilogue

Since I met Sid in 1983 there have been so many changes in the field of firearms.

Many companies copied features of the Detonics Combat Master. Shortened 1911 style pistols appeared from other manufacturers. Companies like Colt, Springfield Armory, Kimber, Sig Sauer, Wilson Combat, S&W, Para Ordnance, Caspian Arms, Auto-Ordnance, STI, High Standard, Charles Daily, Rock Island Armory, Citadel and others followed the innovations started by Detonics.

The "plastic" revolution took place and many manufacturers went to building pistols with polymer receivers. Practical function took a new direction, though aesthetically pleasing classic expressions still have a great following.

The Detonics Combat Master originally turned off some people because of its radical departure from the classic 1911. Thirty years later it is considered a classic beauty and is still a viable fighting pistol.

People will always develop a passion for whatever they will. This is merely human nature. We all decide we like one thing or another and will support our decisions. Those that have a passion for the 1911 have good reason. John Moses Browning created so many of the best firearm designs the world had ever seen. The 1911 was just one of them. The Detonics Combat Master would have made him proud.

Detonics Manufacturing Corporation was purchased by Bruce McCaw in 1987 and became New Detonics. It shortly thereafter moved to Arizona and closed its doors in 1992. In 2004 the third incarnation sprung up in Georgia as Detonics USA. It was headed up by Jerry Ahern. In 2007 all interest of Detonics USA was purchased by Bruce Siddle. Currently the fourth company is known as Detonics Defense and is located in Illinois.

New Detonics Combat Master

Detonics USA Combat Master

Detonics Defense Combat Master

A brief rundown on a few of the original Detonics Manufacturing Corporation Staff:

Richard Niemer is the head gunsmith in charge of Olympic Arms' 1911 division.

Peter Dunn became the Production Engineer at Detonics USA at the Pendergrass plant. He is currently the gunsmith for Champion Arms in Kent, WA.

Nehemiah Sirkis created several rifles and handguns. He worked for Kimber and other companies. He currently continues to design firearms.

Ray Herriott created the Mech Tech CCU (Carbine Conversion Units) for use with 1911 and Glock pistol frames.

Sid's sayings to remember:

1. Remember that the most important person in your life is YOU!
2. A piece of dark chocolate a day will keep the doctor away.
3. I get my daily dose of fruits and vegetables by drinking a glass of red wine.
4. Be sure to always work on something you enjoy!
5. The older I get, the less people I like to be around.
6. Remember to watch your six.

www.ingramcontent.com/pod-product-compliance
Ingram Content Group UK Ltd.
Pitfield, Milton Keynes, MK11 3LW, UK
UKHW041939190726
13854UKWH00004B/1683

9 781105 480768